Djalma Motta Argollo

Evolutionary Possibilities
SPECULATIVE ESSAYS

-2021-

1st Edition

Printed in USA

To my friend Adenauer Novaes

Whose dedication to the study and practice of the Spiritist Doctrine, allied to a deep passion for the souls in conflict, who share with him their existential crises, my friendship and gratitude.

Spiritism is the new science that comes to reveal to men, with irrefutable proof, the existence of the invisible world and its relations with the visible world; it appears to us, no longer as a supernatural thing, but as one of the living forces ceaselessly acting on nature, as the source of a multitude of phenomena, until then misunderstood and rejected, for this reason, for the mastery of the fantastic and the wonderful (KARDEC, 2010, par. 6).

I once talked at length in New York with a friend of William James, Prof. Hyslop, about the matter of proof and identity[1]. He admitted that, taking all the factors into account, the totality of these metaphysics phenomena would be better explained by the spirits' hypothesis rather than by the qualities and peculiarities of the unconscious. Based on my own experiences, I must agree with him on this matter. In each particular case, I must necessarily be skeptical, but in general, I must conceive that the spirits' hypothesis brings better results in practice than any other (JUNG, 2002, p. 35).

Relativistic Physics of the twentieth century did not destroy the concepts of Newtonian physics. It broadened them, considering new paradigms. Such magnification is continuous. It can be said that human knowledge gradually restructures itself, reformulating old hypotheses, which are expressed in a new language. The foundations that formulate new ideas are those that have previously supported human knowledge, but now can be understood in the light of new paradigms. Old concepts or ideas are not despised, as the psyche that reformulates them also rests on them for the sake of discovering other concepts and new ideas (NOVAES, 2004, pp. 21-22).

---

[1] Of the spirits that communicate throughout the mediums. My own explanatory note.

Index

Preface

> *One final characteristic of the Spiritist revelation, and which proceeds from the very conditions in which it is produced, is that, being supported by facts, it cannot help but be essentially progressive like all the sciences of observation. By its essence, it is allied with science, which, being the exposition of the laws of nature through a certain order of facts, cannot be contrary to the will of God, the author of such laws. The discoveries of science glorify God rather than demean God. They destroy only what humans have built upon their erroneous ideas about God.*
>
> *Therefore, Spiritism establishes as an absolute principle only what has been demonstrated by the evidence, or what has arisen logically from observation. Touching on all branches of social economics, to which it lends the support of its own discoveries, it will continue to assimilate all other progressive doctrines of whatever order they may be, which have reached the status of practical truths and which have exited the domain of utopia; otherwise, it would be committing suicide. Ceasing to be what it truly is, it would belie its origin and its providential purpose. Pressing forward with progress, Spiritism will never be surpassed, because if new discoveries were to show it to be in error on one point, it would modify itself on that point. If a new truth is revealed, it accepts it.* (KARDEC, 2011, par. 55).

Only a soul illuminated by the *Spirit of Truth's* lights could define Spiritism, in its evolutionary feature, with so much property. Since March 1958, the lasting contact with The Comforter, made me feel the truth of these hypotheses. In doctrinal practices, through public conferences and debates, with spiritists and, especially, non-spiritists, of all cultural levels, at no time have I had the opportunity to see the Spiritist doctrine even waver, before arguments of whichever nature: philosophical, scientific or religious. On the contrary, I have always witnessed the victory of its logical structure, which offers unbeatable resources to this dialectic that seeks truth. Likewise, I have no knowledge of any scientist that, whatever branch they belonged to (mainly to "eternal repeaters of the obvious branch" in the research field – such as Metaphysics, parapsychology or Psychotronics), might had managed to prove, irretrievably, that any of the spiritists principles are false. I emphasize, however, that I call *spiritist principles* the *survival of the soul*, the existence of the *spiritual world*, the *mediumistic communication* and *reincarnation*.

There is a speculative character to this study of mine, as one can presume from its subtitle. It is not presented as an absolute expression of truth, since this pretension would be boundless, and infinitely ridiculous. Truth is conquered with gradual effort and evolutionary ascension. In addition, all truth is temporary, changeable and always partial. To those who read and disagree with this, I ask of you not to easily criticize. Propose different views of the matter this book approaches, without repeating the obvious over and over again, or voicing opinions with mere *guesswork*.

In 1857, when *The Spirits' Book* was published, the scientific panorama was very narrow. The technological development process was just beginning, and today it reaches a remarkable peak. We lived in a worldview pre-established by the discoveries of Isaac Newton (1642-1727), of an infinite universe in time and space. This scientific belief is now completely outdated. We now know that the universe is finite, both in time and in space. It began in a powerful expansion and it will probably return to the starting point in the compression process, for a bombastic rebirth, in kind of a cosmological reincarnation. Many current astrophysicists claim that the universe will expand until the complete exhaustion of all the stars, absolutely distanced from each other. It would be death by absolute distention of the cosmic tissue. Their thesis is based on the finding, which states that galaxies are escaping much faster, indicating there has been an increasement in prefescape velocity, because of the action of dark matter, the amount of which is estimated at about 84.5% of the total mass of the universe. And it is accelerating the "escape from the galaxies". But this can also be attributed to natural phenomenon that takes place before retraction starts, like the blink of a candle about to consume itself, or the false improvement of the dying.

The Kardecian arguments, based on the Newtonian view of the Cosmos, no longer possess the force that they possessed before, at the time they were formulated. At this point, it is necessary to the spiritist movement an urgent renewal in its scientific vocabulary. It is the process of updating a new scientific conception, proposed by the *Consolidator*[2] of spiritism. This does not mean a defense of the idea that the *Spiritist consolidation*[3] is outdated, or in need of being rewritten. First of all, according to the doctrinal principles, it is not true that the consolidation has been outdated. Secondly, the urge of rewriting the Basic Works themselves is an extravagant proposal under any circumstances. It would be the same as if Plato (428-347 BC) or Aristotle's (384-322 BC) books were rewritten, in order to *update* them. It is absurd since only the authors

---

[2] Term that refers to the work carried out by Allan Kardec, in the structuring of spiritism. Regarding the term *Spiritist consolidation*, from which it derives, see Note number 3.

[3] Term proposed by the spiritist thinker Elzio de Souza Ferreira to replace the term *codification*, in use in the Spiritist movement. The irretrievable argument is that Spiritism is not a code but a set of principles that already exist and are professed by various religions and philosophies, both old and current.

themselves can modify written books. If already disembodied, their work becomes untouchable; they have expressed their thought at a certain historical moment.

Of course, new books can be written, and the concepts of those authors reviewed, criticized and corrected. This is an inalienable right of every human being, and precisely what I am doing with this book: presenting new scientific theories, on top of the scientific concepts of Kardec's work, even if doing so with *speculations*. Regarding the doctrinal part, Kardecian consolidation is monolithic and precise, and our only remaining role would be study it and, naturally, expand and unfold it.

Another interesting point that allows some comments is what I call a *culture of proud repetition*, which has been established amongst many in the spiritist movement. The Spiritist consolidation never intended to be a substitute for definitive truths, ready and finished. Allan Kardec (1804-1869) always emphasized the evolutionary character of Spiritism. Whoever speaks of Evolution, talks about modifications and transformations, as we can see in the epigraph quote in this chapter. It seems to me, however, that some confreres, repeating religious positions of past reincarnations, try to turn the Basic Books *Sacred Scriptures* into a *hagiography*, produced by the divinity itself. This is how statements like this are heard: *Spiritism has an answer to all the questions of Man*. There is nothing more exaggerated. There is a number of questions that remain and will remain without solutions for the time being, and some more time, unless they are provided in the speculative field. For example, Spiritism does not answer the question: is light formed by particles or waves? Nor does it provide the theoretical requirements, which can merge the Theory of Relativity and Quantum Mechanics.

The Spiritist doctrine answers, for sure, the fundamental problems faced by the human being since its origin: *personal immortality, communication with the dead, the generic problem of destiny* and, through *reincarnation*, on some level, to the *goals of the existence*. However, those responses, of different depths, have been a part of the religious and philosophical context of humanity, since time immemorial. In general, they do not belong exclusively to Spiritism, nor were they particularly created by Allan Kardec. What makes the Spiritist doctrine something special in the study of these issues is the *method* it employs, in addition to the conceptual dynamism imprinted in them. Yes, because until Spiritism, reincarnation, for example, was one of the factors that caused *social abulia*, as it was a *necessary religious imposition for the human being to pay for their sins*. Therefore, it generated conformism and allowed the perpetuation of misery and social exploitation, perfect instruments used by the upper ruling social classes in order to keep the people in a perpetual state of subordination to their whims. In order to prove this, it is enough to check the history of India, and of the Eastern regions, where, in general, reincarnation is the belief of the ruling. With Spiritism, the return to life started to be seen as dynamic, progressive and transformative, in its social consequences.

Spiritism is a new kind of knowledge, which predicts a cultural situation that will be in force for centuries to come. It is the beginning of a much deeper and broader process of understanding than the current one. It can be said that the Spiritist doctrine is the vertex of a revolutionary gnosiological angle, which will modify the epistemological parameters to which one was used. I say *was* because, as I have tried to show throughout this book, the emergence of new conceptual paradigms is in motion, as it can be seen according to the study of Relativistic and Quantum Physics, which will reinforce the paradigmatic emergence of psychic concepts, formulated by the Doctrine in a logical and coherent way. In a not-so-distant time, this structural set of knowledge will place the human being before new scientific, philosophical and religious proposals that will subvert current standards, breaking new ground through challenging ideas for scientific thinking. It will be necessary that New Bacons and Descartes propose new and precise methods, capable of meeting the cultural challenges proposed. In the concert of thought, this is, I believe, a more appropriate idea of the doctrine's role: its real contribution to the cultural progress of humanity.

Spiritist knowledge provides the skill to think freely. Its revolutionary axioms, properly proven by experimental research, unlock seductive perspectives on thinking, in a permanent invitation to inquiry and speculation. The Doctrine of free examination and freethinking is not conditioned by dogmas or mysteries of any kind. Even the books of the Spiritist consolidation[4] are open to criticism, as they do not have the pretension of restraining the absolute truth and do not belong to the absurd concept of *inerrancy*, proper to the fanatical thinking of alienating religions. Add to this the fact that the structure of the spiritist movement is not subordinated to any definitive authority, capable of establishing norms and rules of faith, nor any specific controls whatsoever, or a non-spiritist truth. Finally, there is not a court judging what is *doctrinal* or not, even so, because it would be *censorship*, which is incompatible with the freedom of thinking, a basic requirement of a liberating doctrine, such as Spiritism. Only the basic works, or the Spiritist consolidation, have the guiding power, but only in a methodological aspect.

---

[4] *The Spirits' Book, The Medium's Book, The Gospel According to Spiritism, Heaven And Hell* and *Genesis*.

This does not mean that there is a lack of criteria for proving the validity of an idea, whether or not it agrees with the principles of the Doctrine. They exist and were established by the Consolidator:

> *...It is not the opinion of any man which will produce unity*, but the unanimous voices of the Spirits; it will not be any man, least of all myself, who will destroy the Spiritist orthodoxy, neither will it be a Spirit wishing to impose whatever it may be. This unity will be accomplished by the universal gathering of Spirits who communicate throughout the world, by order of God. This is the essential character of the Spiritist Doctrine; this is its force and its authority (KARDEC 2010, p. 23).

Since the beginning of the Consolidation, its touchstone for the veracity of a spiritist proposition is the universal *control of spirits' teaching*. Allan Kardec used it, systematically, and that is the reason why Spiritism is not a personal work, nor will it ever be controlled by individuals or institutions, which in the absence of its own genesis and character, might want to grant themselves such status. Only the fanatical defenders of false spiritual "revelations" have the audacity to reject these common sensed and logical criteria, simply because it contradicts their hallucinations.

The basic works have started a process of knowledge acquisition, the end of which is far from being seen because it will carry on for many and many centuries. Future generations will be responsible for exploiting, on an unimaginable scale, the consequences of their axioms.

This book has as its first goal to demonstrate that there is no incompatibility between the spiritual teachings and contemporary science, with all its conquests. It was born from a seminar held in the *Spiritist Centre Luz e Caridade*, in Salvador, Bahia, under the direction of a dear friend, Leovigildo Santana. At the opportunity, through inspiration, the spirit of Leonardo da Vinci (1452-1519), showed me an interesting model about the interaction between the *Spiritual Universe* and the *Material Universe*. He polarized me with the idea of a Divine Creation, dynamic and oscillating like a pendulum, founding its concepts on the modern achievements of the Physical, Astrophysical and Sciences of Nature. According to him, the spiritual dimensions that unfold in innumerable Universes, deriving from each other, in a continuous gradation, not only in a descending vertical but equally in horizontal in a homogeneous spread. The fundamental point of his thinking is the *gravitational collapse*, validated by *The Theory of Relativity*, due to Einstein's genius, and later deepened from 1970s and on, by Wheller's research, Stephen Hawking (1942-2018), Roger Penrose (1931-...), and others.

According to Leonardo, these dimensional Universes, on a gradual descending scale, create their inferiors, but have no characteristic of Infinity. On the contrary, all of them had a beginning and will have an ending, in a pendular movement of possible permanent character. This refers to the Hindu affirmations on *Brahman's days and nights*, in which contemporary Science seems to revive. It is true, a creation with a beginning and ending does not solve the problem of its initial moment, that is, of the first of all creations. This is another issue and, at the moment, a difficult one to solve. Human directed thinking is analogous and conditioned by the continuum of space-time. It is only possible to think by comparison and sequentially. This hinders an analysis of the phenomena that occur outside of time and space, precisely because there are no elements of comparison in the three-dimensional Universe. However, computer science and, most important, virtual reality's achievements have been teaching the human mind how to penetrate the unusual aspects of metaphysical thought, allowing it to transcend its millennial conditionings. It is a return to the domains of *Metaphysics*, which Cartesian thought tried to dispose of. For centuries, Hindu philosophy has been teaching: everything that exists, in both material and spiritual condition, is a virtual product of God's mind. A mere illusion. And today, in the West, this is a *scientific reality*, thanks to the theory of relativity, quantum physics, chaos theory, information theory, and other many achievements of contemporary science. The third millennium, without any doubt, will witness the meeting of the scientist with the reality of the spirit and, consequently, with Divinity itself. Likewise, scientific research will assimilate *intuition* as an essential working tool, in the search for knowledge, supported by other *mediumistic tools*, which Spiritism studies and propagates. Essentially, this is what I will approach in the following pages.

I also took the opportunity to speculate on other subjects, such as *evolution*, *ectoplasm*, *perispirit* and *mediumship*. Regarding specialized information of relativistic and quantum physics, which are not my area of primary interest, the books used to research are quoted in the text and appear in the *bibliographic sources*.

1. EVOLUTION AND SPIRITISM

A draft on the Progress of Psychic Sciences

In the nineteenth century, science had been going through a revolution, transforming all previously established knowledge; simultaneously, another new paradigm was under development: Spiritism, arising from old facts that wise men once labeled as superstition, had been asserting itself as a new source of knowledge, changing traditional concepts about beings and things.

Spirits unfold a new and important object for research, which transforms all previously established knowledge when it proves that life goes on after the physical death crisis. The existence of other and new dimensions started being discussed, mainly because they interact with our systematic form, acting on all the phenomena traditionally studied.

This Science also had its historical development marked by notable discoveries. On March 31st of 1848, Margaret Fox discovers that spirits can produce physical phenomena, in this specific case, noises (raps) and, through them, communicate with the people from this world. Duesler then developed a method that allowed the association of raps with the letters of the alphabet, later perfected by David Fox and Isaac Post, who placed mediums and assistants around a table to systematically develop a mediumistic meeting for the first time. All of this in 1848. Jonathan Koons and his family, in 1852, started holding effective meetings of physical effects, with a research laboratory and creation of the first phosphorescent chemical elements and instruments responsible for facilitating the production of phenomena. Robert Hare (1781-1858) applies methods and Physics' instruments in studies and experiments related to mediumistic facts, proving the reality surrounding them (see ARGOLLO, 1994).

Under the pseudonym Allan Kardec, Professor Hippolyte Léon Denizard Rivail, deepened the study of the spirit, systematizing its teachings and revelations in a logical and solid doctrinal body, to which he gave the name of Spiritism. He was the only researcher able to glimpse the spiritual matter in all its magnitude and depth, as well as establish the fundamental principles and laws in the study and exercise of mediumship, as something that exists within spiritual evolution; he is just as important to the studies of destiny and the human soul as Einstein, Freud, Jung, Plato, Aristotle and Immanuel Kant, gathered together. The German Johann Karl Friedrich Zöllner (1834-1882), proved the *fourth-dimension* theory, after studying the physical effects phenomena, where he was able to verify the penetrability of matter-by-matter, under the action of disembodied spirits. Frederic William Henry Myers (1843-1901) founded, in 1882, the Society for Psychical Research – SPR, alongside William Fletcher Barret (1845-1926), Edmund Gurney (1847-1888), Henry Sidgwick (1838-1900), and others, initiating properly verified researches and popular inquiries on mediumistic phenomena.

One of the great names in nineteenth-century Physics, William Crookes, consolidated the evidence on the continuity of life after death in memorable studies that took place in his laboratory, where he experimented with mediums Daniel Dunglas Home (1833-1886) and Florence Cook. The Italian philosopher Ernesto Bozzano (1862-1943) produced magnificent monographs, to which he applied the convergence of proof method, demonstrating that mediumship is an unconscious faculty, the externalization of the self's senses towards the spiritual *habitat*.

When studying medium Kathleen Goligher, W. J. Crawford (who died in 1930), the Mechanical Engineering professor at the Queen's University Belfast, makes the following discoveries: a) that during the physical effects phenomena, the medium's body undergoes weight variations; b) that, when materializations or the movement of objects occur, ectoplasm is projected from the medium's body as if it was a bar of varying size acting as a lever, now called *Crawford lever*. Sir William James (1842-1910), North American philosopher and psychologist, studied Psychophony mediumship alongside R. Hodgson, F. Myers, Oliver Lodge (1851-1940), W. F. Barret and Mrs. Sidgwick (1845-1936), and the medium Eleonora Piper, managing to gather enough evidence on the veracity of the phenomenon.

Eugene Auguste Albert de Rochas D'Aiglun (1837-1914), head of the Paris Polytechnic School, studied reincarnation through regression, using hypnosis. Likewise, he managed to externalize the human double and, consequently, motor skills, contributing to a better understanding of the physical effects phenomena.

William McDougall laid the foundation for the creation of the Parapsychology Laboratory at the University of Duke. In charge, Joseph Banks Rhine, who developed and applied to telepathy, clairvoyance and psychokinesis phenomena the statistical method of probabilities, proving them exhaustively. In order to do that, Dr. Rhine applied tests with the Zenner deck, which contains five suits of five simple figures: the plus signal, stylized waves, square, circle and star. Automatically shuffled, the cards are submitted to the experiments' subjects, according to the phenomena under study. For telepathy, they are viewed by the emitter, as the receiver tries to capture them, in synchrony, by writing their perceptions of the figures in a specific form, which is then confronted with that of the emitter and a control; regarding the clairvoyance test in the future, they are first guessed, then shuffled and checked the same way; for those of pure clairvoyance, they are shuffled and the percipient seeks to capture their order through the same process. In the psychokinesis case, many different kinds of data are, in general, used, mixed and automatically launched, while the subject tries to act mentally on them to make them show one of the faces previously chosen.

In Italy, the medium Pietro Ubaldi transmitted the following concept, from an entity so-called *Your Voice*:

> In speaking of progressive truths, I have also extended such concept of relativity to psychology and philosophy.
> Just as it has to be done with the evolutionist concept, which Darwin observed in the organic species only, so the concept of relativity, which Einstein confined to a few mathematical moments, must be completed with a theory of universal relativity that should be extended to the whole universe. This represents a philosophical and scientific conquest, a more profound concept, a broader understanding, a loftier beauty and harmony. Another in-depth concept of relativity can be expanded: the one that will lead you to new concepts, no more just the ones on the relativity of the measuring units of your universe, but a much greater and more profound one on the evolution of their dimensions. (Ubaldi,1959, pp. 144-145).

And this happened in 1933 when Einstein was still a controversial subject in the Physics field.

It was in Sweden, on June 12, 1959, that the most important phenomenon until this day in the mediumistic area stated: Instrumental Transcommunication – ITC. That day, Friedrich Jüergenson, Russian artist, a naturalized Sweden citizen, recorded spiritual voices on a magnetic tape. It was the realization of Thomas Alva Edison, Gugliemo Marconi, Nikola Tesla, Augusto Cambraia, Cornélio Pires and other pioneers' dreams. On the same path, George Meek created the Spiricom (Spirit Communication), in the USA, a device that allowed him to talk to spirits, and the result was presented to the public in 1982.

In 1983, Hans Otto König, creator of the *Generator* – an apparatus similar to the Spiricom –, held communication with the Beyond in a live radio show, in Luxembourg, and later repeated the successful attempt on Luxembourg TV, also live, on 24 January 1986.

But the researchers brought up new ways of communication with the spirits. In 1976, in the United States, Scott Rogo and Raymond Bayless conducted studies about mediumistic communication via telephone, known as calls from the beyond, verifying that they had been happening for quite some time and in a disseminated way.

In Germany, Klaus Schreiber, in 1984, recorded the first images of spirits on television, starting the Videocom, mediumistic communications on-screen, filmed by video cameras. In 1982, also in Germany, Manfred Boden received the first spiritual messages via personal computer, in an *electronic obsession* case. In Brazil, Dr. Hernani Guimarães Andrade founded the Brazilian Institute of Psychobiophysical Research – IBPP, and his works in the field of Poltergeist, reincarnation and Kirlian photography (the creator of colored Kirlian photography) are known worldwide; he also launched the *Corpuscular Theory of the Spirit*, with remarkable success in the generation of instruments and incentives for Psychic Studies. In a later issue, the title was changed to *Quantum Psi*.

Dr. Jorge Andréa dos Santos raised the structure of the unconscious, demonstrating that the spirit is a complex set of functions in transit towards an unimaginable future; his works provided the theoretical foundation for a profound review of traditional psychiatry and psychology. Naturally,

I failed to mention numerous researchers and achievements of mediumistic studies from all times. But the sample allows me to demonstrate how much has already been done in this field, which preludes the achievements of the future.

Psychology, Physics and Biology are led to review all their fundamental axioms, expanding their areas as well as finding an answer to previously unsolvable problems, as we will try to show in the course of this essay. In Psychology, the Swiss psychiatrist Carl Gustav Jung (1875-1961) initiated a reformulation of Freud's concept about the unconscious, expanding the knowledge dimension of the human psyche. His discovery of the *collective unconscious* and *archetypes* became the basis to unravel myths and, consequently, the human being's structural ways of thinking. Jung created Analytical Psychology, which is much more than a therapeutic method; it is a method that allows human beings to develop their psychic potentialities. His studies also covered mediumistic phenomena, the ones that happened amongst his ancestors on the mother's side, with his mother, with himself. His doctoral thesis focused on the mediumistic phenomena that had occurred with a cousin of his, in meetings he had led for two years. Finally, numerous patients reported the occurrence of mediumistic phenomena, which he immortalized in his writings (see ARGOLLO, 2004).

Evolutionary Development

Evolution was the nineteenth century's great discovery. Just like gravity, the effects of which men have always known and used, but were only explicitly described by Isaac Newton, the evolutionary process has always exerted its action on beings and things of our planet, but it only found an actual definition in the last century.

Through the ages, some thinkers predicted the concept of evolution, usually attached to specific cases, in brief reasoning. With the development of geological studies, especially those after Lyell, the slow process of planetary crust formation was discovered. Fossil remains were found in a complex ascending sequence in the structural layers of the soil.

Biological knowledge derived from comparative analysis and the search for a phytozoological classification, as complete as possible – Tournefort (1656-1708), Linneu (1707-1778) A. L. de Jussieu (1748-1836) --, allowed the idea of evolution to present itself more and more strongly to scientific thought. However, the academic circles would greatly resist this theory, since the axioms of *spontaneous generation* and *periodic catastrophism* were in display – it should be noted that this theory, after some modifications, was revived at the end of the last century. Many thinkers, alongside religious leaders of the time, feared that the abandonment of these concepts would tear down the ruling ethical structures, implying social breakdown, the implantation of Anarchism, the subversion of order. Nevertheless, evolution is a fact, and there are no arguments against facts. Evolution was gradually imposing itself, at first in the anthropological and sociological view, even before Charles Robert Darwin (1809-1882), with his book: *The Origin of Species*. David Hume (1711-1776), the creator of phenomenist philosophy, and Adam Smith (1703-1790), Scottish economist, both elaborated their theories from the Evolutionist concept of human society; Auguste Comte (1798-1857), the creator of Positivism, had his concepts permeated by evolutionism. Karl Marx (1818-1857) and Friedrich Engels (1820-1895) elaborated the historical materialism thesis on an evolutionary foundation. Herbert Spencer (1820-1903), intellectual inspirer of the famous spiritist Ernesto Bozzano (1862-1943), was, in our opinion, the philosopher who best expressed the new way of analyzing man and society, according to a continuing and gradual view of progress.

In Biology, Jean Baptiste Lamarck (1744-1829) indicated an animal evolutionary theory and laws on the hereditary aspect and inheritance of acquired characteristics. However, it was Darwin, in his cited book released on 24 November 1859, who unleashed the great battle for the introduction of evolution into human culture, to the extent that he discovered its basic mechanism: natural selection. Although Darwin's undeniable merit has to be shared with Alfred Russel Wallace (1823-1913), who came to the same conclusion and term, the law of Natural selection, at the same time and independently. Later on, Wallace started to study mediumistic phenomena, and then became a great and passionate advocate of life's continuity beyond the grave, thanks to the facts he had raised in hundreds of serious and unassailable experiences. Herbert Wendt, in his *Ich Suchte Adam,* translated under the title *In Search of Adam*, writes about this fact, with blatant irony: *After Darwins's death, one of his paladins deserted him. Wallace took up spiritualism and came to believe more in table tuning and prophetic mediums than in the intelligence of orangutans and nature's skill in breeding* (Wendt, 1956, pp. 266).

The truth is that Wallace had studied spiritual phenomena long before Darwin's death, applying to them the same observation and analysis criteria that led him to the Natural Selection discovery, in parallel to the English naturalist, which reassures his conclusions in the psychic Sciences area.

Spiritism: An Evolutionary Doctrine

Two years before Darwin's *The Origin of Species* had been released, *The Spirits' Book* emerged, in Paris on April 18, 1857, signed by Hippolyte-Léon Denizard Rivail, under the pseudonym Allan Kardec, whose intelligence and pedagogical ability was recognized in the City of Lights. Like Wallace, Professor Rivail had been led to the study of mediumistic phenomena due to the arrival of the rotating tables, or dance of the tables, as they were then known, popular in the bourgeois French halls. Examining it in a systematic and methodical way, without prejudice, he acquired the conviction of survival after death.

> The first event to be observed was the movement of various objects, popularly called table-turning or the dance of the tables. This phenomenon appears to have been first observed in America (or rather, it recurred in that country, since history shows that it actually dates back to remote antiquity (KARDEC, 2007, pp. 18-19).

I assure this phenomenon has had the merit of polarizing the attention of genius men towards the larger problem of the spirit's existence. Putting his privileged brain and his polymorphic culture at the disposal of emergent knowledge, Kardec began to observe and classify the facts, as well as to inquire them in order to discover their origin, function and goals. That is because, within the spiritist phenomenon, there are faculties of own intelligence and will, because they are produced by intelligent incorporeal beings, that is, unprovided with a somatic body, and are nothing more than the souls of dead men.

As for new facts, new methods must be applied, Allan Kardec, realizing the rational ability of spiritist phenomena's agents, led them to define themselves and, through an inter-dimensional dialogue, in which many mediums took part, he managed to collect a vast amount of material that, under his criteria, organizing and systematizing abilities, became a compendium for spiritualist Philosophy: *The Spirits' Book*. An evolutionary view of Man lays within it, both from the physical and the spiritual point of view:

> It has been stated that the human soul at its origin resembles the state of human infancy in the corporeal life, that its intelligence is only beginning to unfold, and that it is preparing itself for life (see no. 190). Where does the soul accomplish this primary phase?
> In a series of existences preceding the period you call humanity.
>
> Then it would seem that the soul had been the intelligent principle of the lower beings of creation; correct?
> Haven't we stated that everything in nature is linked together and tends toward unity? It is in those beings, whom you are far from knowing about entirely, that the intelligent principle is developed, is gradually individualized and is prepared for life, as we have stated. In a certain way, it is a preparatory work like that of germination, after which the intelligent principle undergoes a transformation and becomes a spirit. It is then that the period of humanity begins for it, and with it the consciousness of its future, the distinction between good and evil and the responsibility for its acts – the same way that childhood comes before adolescence, then youth and finally adulthood. There is nothing humiliating about this origin. Do the greatest geniuses feel humiliated at having been shapeless fetuses in the maternal womb? If anything ought to humiliate them it is their low status before God and their powerlessness to probe the depths of the divine designs and the wisdom of the laws regulating the harmony of the universe. Strive to realize the greatness of God in the admirable harmony that establishes the solidarity of all things in nature. To believe that God could have made anything without a purpose, and have created intelligent beings without a future, would be to blaspheme God's goodness, which The Three Kingdoms extends over all creatures. (KARDEC, 2007, question 607).

One should emphasize that this evolutionary-biological positioning of the Consolidating spirits contradicted Kardec's thinking, adept of the spontaneous generation, theory that at his time had the same universal acceptance as the theory of evolution has today. I call Consolidating spirits those who participated, at any level, in the systematization of Spiritist consolidation, alongside the incarnated team: Allan Kardec and the mediums.

As mentioned before, Spiritism had predicted physical and spiritual evolutionism two years before, even providing a justifiable and rational basis for the doctrine. The spirit appeared as a register center of the biological changes, a place to fixate acquired characters, as well as the organizing and managing matrix of the organism and its functions.

Leon Denis and Gabriel Delanne immediately continued Allan Kardec's work, and Leon Denis' view on evolution is evident in his book *After Death*, where he states that in the lower domains of creation, the being still ignores itself. Instinct alone and necessity drive it, and it is only in the more evolved types that, like a pale dawn, the first rudiments of the faculties appear. In humanity, the soul comes to its moral freedom. Its judgment and its consciousness develop more and more, as it travels through its great journey (DENIS, 1977, pp. 324).

He also mentioned that, in the Universe, everything evolves and tends to a higher, transforming and perfectioning state. From the depths of the abyss, life rises, often confused, indecisive, animating innumerable forms, ever more perfect; then, it expands into the human being, where it acquires consciousness, reason, freedom, constituting the soul or spirit (DENIS, 1977, pp. 428). Furthermore, Dr. Delanne states that it is through an uninterrupted evolution, from the most rudimentary forms of life, until the human condition, that the thinking principle slowly conquers its individuality (DELANNE, 1976, p. 16). Still in the *Introduction*, when approaching the goals of the book, he wondered: despite the permanent flow of matter that renews the organism all the time, where does the individual and typical fixity of living beings come from? Such are the first questions that we propose to solve, at times referring to the perispirit in our research (DELANNE, 1976, pp. 18). Further on, he continued affirming that the immortal agent who animates all beings is always one, whole, and unique. From the beginning, it manifests itself in the most rudimentary forms, however, in the last stages of life it goes on improving little by little, at the same time that it rises on the scale of beings. In this long evolution, it develops latent faculties and manifests them more or less identical to ours, as it approaches humanity (DELANNE, 1976, p. 74).

Palingenesis and Evolution

Palingenesis or reincarnation is an important factor in the evolutionary process. It is a mechanism that allows the spiritual being to repeat their experiences *ad infinitum*, recording the results within the spiritual body, and thus, increasingly evolving in its complexity and allowing greater stages of progress. The Consolidating spirits thus expressed themselves regarding the theme:

> How can a soul who did not reach perfection during its corporeal life complete the work of its purification? By submitting to the trial of a new existence (KARDEC, 2007, question 166).
>
> Then does the soul live many corporeal existences? Yes, we all live many lives and those who say otherwise wish to keep you in the ignorance in which they themselves dwell. That is their desire (KARDEC, 2007, 2nd supplement to question 166).

The Law of Reincarnation, being a law of Nature, is based on God's righteousness, like all laws. Regarding the subject, the Consolidator comments:

> The doctrine of reincarnation, which consists in accepting the fact that humans have many successive lives, is the only one that is in line with the idea of God's justice concerning those of a lower moral condition. It is the only one that can explain our future and give us hope because it offers us the means of atoning for our errors through new trials. Reason confirms this and it is what the Spirits have taught us (KARDEC, 2007, question 171, Kardec's comments).

During the recurrence of numerous experiences in the physical plane, beings are organized, both from a physical and a psychic standpoint. This organization reflects in their group experiences, in social and cultural dimensions. This is possible due to the existence of a permanent dimension juxtaposed to ours: the spiritual universe, which Allan Kardec also called the spiritual world or Erraticity. It is the *habitat* of spirits in the interval of reincarnations, the region from which we came and where we will return after the denouement.

The psychic cosmos and the physical cosmos live in constant interaction, in a constant exchange of energetic impulses. We will return to explore the links between those two-dimensional complexes, in their genetic structural aspect, when we ponder over universal evolution. There is an exchange established between both planes that allows the spirit to experiment the two recurring cyclical realities, imprinting specific qualities, which produce constant and determined improvement.

As a natural phenomenon, reincarnation is a spontaneous action, as well as. There is a basic law, or set of laws, that determines the end of the errant spirits' intermission period, just as an organic cycle determines the end of animated beings' biological trajectory. Or it may be that the moment of the meeting between the male and female gametes creates, as theorized Dr. Hernani Guimarães Andrade, a biomagnetic field that attracts the spiritual entity, which has an affinity bond with the possible mother, nearby.

Since the spirits are the *souls of men who lived on Earth*, of course one must take into account their mental behavior towards the rebirth phenomenon, which can generate interferences during the process of reincarnation, modifying the automatic cycle. Similarly to what living scientists do, intervening in the automatic gestation process, accompanying the fetus' development in the maternal womb in order to detect diseases and provide treatments, allowing a normal development of the pregnancy. Just like that, spirits experts in reincarnation can assist the reincarnating spirit, helping it to accomplish its goals. However, this is not a rule, but an exception. Nowadays, there has been an increasement in generic engineering, so it is natural for these studies to exist also in the *spiritual world*, where all things begin. After all, our greatest scientists had been there before they incarnated.

Perhaps that is why, in the second half of the last century, a movement, which intended to acquire greater knowledge and control of embryological facts, was developed. It allowed the modification of genetic codes in chromosomes, acting upon Human Fertilization, executing it outside the body, in test tubes, with subsequent implantation of the modified egg cell, into the maternal womb, or into a surrogate. Further progress in this area has been achieved with the production of human clones, artificially duplicating the natural process by which Nature produces monozygotic twins.

The mediumistic revelations of long ago have already told us that *Spiritual Geneticists* plan reincarnations, designing organisms in minimal detail, for spirits that need to perform specific work on Earth. *A priori*, spiritual scientists can draw the future body, and the prospective spirit to reincarnate is able to interfere in the project, requesting changes that they deem necessary (XAVIER, 1991, Ch. 12).

Genetic Engineering beckons with the possibility of meddling in the early stages of intrauterine life, to overcome genetic pathologies and, even, sex alterations in the fetus. We see, therefore, that there is nothing extraordinary in the possibility that, in the spiritual universe immediate to the Earth, similar work is carried out, there is much more time and depth, because it is directed according to ethical principles grounded in evangelical axioms.

The test-tube baby, frozen embryos, artificial insemination, human cloning, and so on all of them produced in the genetic field to facilitate human reproduction, represent the Superior spirituality's response to the fallacious works on birth control suggested by questionable, and usually dishonest, economic policies, policies that must suit the population, not the other way around.

Reincarnation Planning and Evolution

Concerning *reincarnation planning* that exists in centers of the spiritual world, one must remain alert against a simplistic belief that *all* reincarnations are *planned*. Well, such an idea is absurd. The very rates of births in the world each day are an obstacle to it. Being a natural law, it occurs with no need for help. But it does not prevent possible cases of planned reincarnations, such as that of spirits who have missions of interest to social groups, and even for all mankind. Naturally, they are provided with biological and existential resources, so that their missions are accomplished with minimum distortions.

In more common cases, however, there may not be any planning, or the planning may be incomplete, deprived of further and deeper studies on historical and social facts that may have a detrimental effect on what the reincarnating spirit is proposing to perform. In addition, erroneous beliefs can be on the basis of planning, compromising it in whole or in part.

Here is an example of a simplistic reincarnation planning in André Luiz's work. The spiritual author tells that the family he had in his last incarnation left the physical body in deplorable moral conditions, except for his mother and a sister, who had disembodied as a child. His grandfather remained for years in the lower spiritual world, amongst richness hallucinatory visions. One of his sisters remained disturbed in the spiritual regions immediate to the crust. His father, when incarnated, had been linked to prostitutes, and many of them waited for him in the "regions of death", two of which remained linked to him, as he could not detach himself from them in order to change his "reality level". It is clear that he did not change due to his own unwillingness, since each of us is responsible for our own situation. Blaming others for one's own misguided choices is comfortable, but it is a false apology. André Luiz himself spent eight years wandering in the densest spiritual regions. After he was able to raise his vibratory pattern, he then changed to the "reality level" where a spiritual city called "Our Home" is located. Sometime later, his mother, who belonged to a different "reality level", told him a plan to "save" her husband, his father, along with the two women with whom he had been involved. He would reincarnate, directly from the primary "reality level" where he was. Then she would reincarnate. Both would then meet and remarry in the future. The plan would be complete with the reincarnation of the two spirits who had remained in the lower spirituality. The plan had been exposed, she said, to "her superior," and they had approved it "for the inferior could not rise to the superior, but the superior could descend to the inferior and rescue him". André Luiz's grandmother was the "sister who had died when he was still a child", and she had already reincarnated. It was a perfect plan. And André Luiz's mother, expected, in the end, to return with all three of them redeemed.

Analyzing: firstly, it is not stated that the three objectives of the plan: the husband and the two mistresses had been previously consulted and had agreed to it. On the contrary, it is said that the husband had no desire to change levels, and the two women did not even want that. Note that the characters of the former family are still treated as members of that same family. And more, it gives the impression that everything remained and would remain as in the past. And this impression does not come only from this particular case. In the same book (XAVIER, 1988, chaps. 47-48), a lady called Laura, who is about to reincarnate, is introduced, and her "husband" had already reincarnated and had been waiting for her, to start a family again... Nevertheless, moving forward, according to the spiritual author, this happened at the end of 1939, and the reincarnations of André's both parents took place, therefore, in 1940. A problem that needs to be immediately addressed is the fact that the two female spirits would remain in the spiritual world, while the male, to whom they were attached by strong sexual ties, would reincarnate. Did no one think that he would suffer a serious sexual obsession? He was already used to intense activity in this area, even in a time of great repression, like that of the previous life. Thus, of course, he would be very open to the spiritual influence of old partners. More important yet is the fact that he would complete twenty years old in the early 1960s, when sexual liberation had started alongside a whole rebel movement of young people. It completely altered the relationship between sexes in western society. By this time, in the same decade, ex-husband and ex-wife would be getting married again and the two entities would probably reincarnate. Imagine that two spirits, used to a life of prostitution, would be living in times when women were liberated by the invention of the birth control pill. At a time when women were extremely repressed, they had become prostitutes. After, they returned to the physical body, without any signs of behavior change, in the middle of the sexual revolution era. Imagine what they would not be doing... In fact, the venture was doomed to go wrong or at least not achieve the desired goal. The question that remains is, was the plan born of an act of extreme love or, on the contrary, of a guilt complex on the part of the ex-wife? Is it possible that she would, unconsciously, blame herself for the fact that the ex-husband had sought sex in the brothels of his time? Moreover, who can guarantee that the author of the plan would successfully go through the whirlwind of the sixties? For me, the plan must not have achieved the expected goals, but, either way, the experience should have been worth it, as everything points out that the characters are still embodied. As the popular saying tells: man proposes, God disposes.

Much is said in mediumistic literature about spirits who have incarnated with socially limited missions but "deviated themselves", not fulfilling the commitments enthusiastically accepted. Perhaps one should consult *The Spirits' Book*, where there is a logical explanation about such "failures": there are spirits who ask for missions that are beyond their means, and therefore cannot accomplish what they intended. The problem is not, as psychographic works by Brazilian mediums presume, due to the spirits "getting carried away by evil suggestions", but rather the result of an erroneous assessment of the possibilities from those same spirits regarding the achievements of the intended goal. In this case, the failure cannot be attributed exclusively to the spirit who has requested the opportunity, but also to those who have agreed to the project. After all, either there was not a correct assessment of the spirit's possibilities, or, in fact, nothing was evaluated. I am ready to conceive that the possibility of failure might have been interpreted as a learning factor. Thus, failure or thrive have the same pedagogical value for the spirit, which can restart, at a new opportunity, what was not accomplished, after all, *death does not exist.*

But what is it that imposes reincarnation as an evolutionary necessity? To answer this question, one must understand the spirits' life after disincarnation, in the Erraticity. The attraction of a spirit to a particular person or group of people is subordinated to a well-known psychological law: *the psychological affinity law.* Thus, according to spiritist principles, in the *spiritual plane*, or in *erraticity*, spirits gather in cohesive groups, which are formed according to the set of feelings and similar trends of their components. These groups are of extraordinarily strong psychological cohesion and impose on their elements a behavioral inertia. The tendency to the similarity of the group's behavior implies a great difficulty in finding reactive opposition, the only way to promote a need for individual change. This is because only the different ones can cause mutual changes.

According to Sociology, human society is external to man and exerts pressure on him. This axiom applies with greater intensity to spiritual societies. There, social coercion is of such intensity, that it imposes a form of standardized behavior. The peculiarity of spiritual existence is a contributor factor; there the unconscious concretely projects itself in the environment, revealing the intimate life of the spirit. Thus, its thoughts and emotions become clear to all the surroundings.

There can be no greater repressive element than this: the systematic and unavoidable exposure of the intimate life. Undoubtedly, in spiritual societies, moral equilibrium is a consequence of great repression of the personality's "negative" aspects towards the *shadows*. To a certain extent, the result is an artificial virtuosity as the repressed contents have not been resolved and continue putting pressure on the conscious. That is why, sometimes, in these societies, spirits begin to suffer, having various symptoms such as nightmares, anxieties, indefinite malaise, depression, etc. Such episodes provide a tension between the conscious and the unconscious, brought about by the unilateral aspect in which conscious life is developing, and that needs to be resolved.

Note that through Francisco Cândido Xavier's mediumistic descriptions, or through the mediums that were influenced by him, the spirits living in morally balanced spiritual societies are panicked before the requirement to reincarnate, which is easy to understand, because it is very good to live in a community where everyone is striving to maintain a high standard of ethical behavior. But the problem is that their speeches on the problem of reincarnation are saturated with defense mechanisms, by which they divert the real focus of the problem, because they refer to the possibilities of "returning to the old and harmful habits", as if the fault laid in the physical body, and not in themselves. The repressed "evil", they sense, will tend to make itself present in their future physical existence, not by a Machiavellian imposition of the unconscious, nor because "matter is an evil", but by the need for recognition and *integration* of this "evil". Only then an effective transformation, or Metanoia, will be possible, when the so-called Machiavellian contents are able to integrate the consciousness, and its energy made available for individual growth.

When incarnated, the spirit has better conditions to "see" its own *shadow*, thanks to the projections made by the unconscious about individuals and events of their everyday reality. One can draw an analogy with the discoveries of nuclear physics, when scientists focused on the result of subatomic particles' *projection*, accelerated by a *cyclotron*, in a *bubble chamber*. The particles themselves are not seen, but the drawings from their trajectories allow fruitful inferences about them. Just as that, the *projections of the unconscious* allow each individual to become aware of his or her real personality, overcoming the resistance imposed by the *ego's defense mechanisms*. In addition, this would be practically impossible in a spiritual society, where one-sided conscience is followed by the Hebrew-Christian tradition of making *evil* a *bad* product of free will. This problem will be analyzed further below.

In conclusion, reincarnation allows the spirit to be alone with itself and, without having its intimate easily and completely deranged, and to be able to work, in a relative *inner loneliness*, their psychic contents. And this thanks to the permanent psychophysical "friction" with the environment where existence occurs, limited by innumerable material and psychic constraints, which lead it to expand its self-knowledge ability, allowing, because of this, its self-transformation.

Evolution and Free Will

When one points to a teleological purpose of the Spirit's great evolutionary process, one immediately questions free will, for without freedom there could be no individual responsibility.

It is clear that in the matter level there can be no free will, because its constituting elements, much like itself, are subject to incoherent and inflexible laws. Particles, atoms and molecules follow schemes determined by physicochemical laws, behaving within blind automatism, easily verifiable. However, there already are wise people who intend to find Will and choice in subatomic particles. All of the material manifestations, since the quark (or even before it), would have intelligence in fullness within themselves, for they have a spiritual principle, but their manifestation would be subordinated to the possibility of expression, proposed by the demonstration vehicle used by this principle (see SMITH, 1975). Some nuclear physicists intend to find a diminutive ability of choice in the electron, when it interacts, which would demonstrate, in addition to intelligence, free will. For me, however, the psyche that lays under the matter would be, just as matter itself, subordinated to strict laws, which do not allow it to exercise free will, but direct it deterministically.

Among the inferior plants and animals, there is full subordination to biological laws, although one can verify clear trials of choice. Among superior animals, the process of analysis and selection is much more developed, although instinct predominates widely. Only man has an unquestionable ability for free choice.

As the spirit reaches the ego consciousness, it gradually becomes responsible for the consequences of its actions. In addition, with reason overlapping the blind instinct, it begins to act on the world as a transformative and creator. With the growth of intellectual skill, it is able to understand itself and nature, always more and more, bending the ridges of wisdom. However, intellectual evolution is much faster than moral evolution therefor causing friction, while coexisting, while coexisting. This friction can be translated as a deviant behavior, generator of acute suffering that imposes itself.

Basically, the problem of free will implies the problem of evil. Religious people, in general, consider evil as a byproduct of the human being's free will. One should meditate Carl Gustav Jung's replica to Erich Fromm, when he defended evil as an "invention" of man, as is done, even, within the spiritist movement: "Who created the serpent?" The spiritists would have to ask: How is it possible that evil is a human creation if God, an omniscient being, that is, who knows everything even in the smallest details, both from the past, the present and the future, created the spirits Himself, even though He knew that they would err, committing various evils? I mean, when God created the spirit that once incarnated as Hitler, for example, He knew, before its creation, everything it would do, including the crimes of genocide and cruel tortures during the Second Great War. The question that remains is, if God knew that Hitler would do what he did, where is the *freedom of choice*? In this case, as in all of them, there is no possibility of doing evil, but the *certainty* that he would, for God *knows in advance what has been done*. Which means, Hitler did what He wanted to be done, and did not *choose* what he could do. That is where the so-called *God's attributes* lead us, which in truth are qualities that we *ascribed* to Him. Is it not time to review these *attributions*?

The greatest restriction on freedom of action lies in the human being's psyche itself; it is the conflict that arises from events which take place during the existence, the interaction with the environment. This activity often generates behavioral restrictions, a natural product of unilateralizations in the field of consciousness, produced by one's self-limiting perception of the world. The consciousness unilaterality, in general, is produced by psychic adaptations that the individual is compelled to put into practice, because of the environment in which they live. Therefore, they generate beliefs and, in turn, behaviors, which can lead to the establishment of various psychopathologies, of varying degrees, which provide self-inflicted limitations, equally in diverse gradation.

With this rapid analysis, one can attest that there can be no absolute freedom of action within a being who finds itself in permanent transformation. Yes, there is a constant conquest of freedom spaces, subordinated to an increasing responsibility, which is its inseparable function. Full freedom of choice and action can only own the spirit that has reached absolute equilibrium; it breaks evolutionary grounds beyond dense matter. After all, said Jesus: *And ye shall know the truth, and the truth shall make you free* - Jo 8: 32).

The evolved spirit, perfectly intertwined with the Creation's goals, which the spirit is not yet able to see, fulfills itself as it pleases, because, due to its integration with the great principles of the Being, it can never cause distortions that lead to disharmony and chaos. Moreover, if it does so, it is for a definite purpose, a need for a project that will be developed, or in which it will come to interfere.

According to the spirits that communicate with us, the spirit that we know by the name of Jesus, a name that was given to him when he incarnated among us, is responsible for the *Earth project*, that is, for the creation of an orb where spiritual protoforms and spirits themselves evolve. If that is the case, one can observe that, from the human point of view, its evolutionary design is based on the *conflict of opposites*, where the *Law of Destruction* is a preponderant factor. There is a permanent conflict between beings and the environment, which creates painful obstacles that have to be beaten hard; similarly, beings are divided between predators and preys, a requirement from the *Conservation Law*. For me to live, I must kill and consume a living being, animal and/or plant. That is, in the earthly evolutionary process, life feeds life, even though this is the cause of pain and unrestrained violence. The *struggle for life* is an imposition from which we cannot escape yet. Even vegetarians are included in the process of *food violence* because they also kill and cause suffering in order to stay alive. After all, many experiments lead us to believe that plants have the ability to feel, therefore pointing to the assumption that their destruction is a violence since it causes them suffering. However, this aspect of evolution, which seems to be evil, by the intensity of suffering that it produces, generates good, which is the continuous improvement of beings and things. One cannot forget that an *evolved spirit* is the one who has reached a degree of *individualization* that allows it to balance itself between opposites, in the psyche's plane. At this stage, both *good* and *evil*, in the inner field, are solved definitively (from what one can imagine), by the *transcendent function*, which provides it with full knowledge of itself, its motivations and, consequently, of the other same level spirits, and even from inferior ones.

Jesus is an example of what I have just said, since he could identify both goodness and evil, amongst his fellow citizens, in a simple, direct and equidistant way.

Non-Spiritist Evolutionary Models

The Hindu Model

I do not believe that one can truly speak of an evolutionary theory of the spirit among Hindus. Even when they admit the passage of the spirit through the realms of nature, the meaning of this path is different from what we call evolution.

For Spiritism, the intelligent principle, created by God, comes from a state in which it is *simple and ignorant*, unprovided with prior knowledge or development, other than a *genetic* tendency for improvement, or rather, a quantum of virtues, capable of growing, and that is the decisive factor for everyone for achieving perfection.

Hinduism, however, claims that the Atman, or spirit, was created in all its plenitude of wisdom and perfection. But how to justify that there are so many problems and distortions in the life of these souls? Simple. When created, the spirits are thrown to the webs of Maya, the goddess of illusion. Then, they lose their fundamental identity, which is linked to the creator and to all creatures, and they start to have the dichotomy's *separateness deliriums*. Not only the Spirit, but also all that exists, is disconnected from the set where they live. While enduring this illusion, the soul will pass through the realms of nature, bending variegated bodies and experiencing the most diverse situations.

The situation only comes to an end when ignorance ceases, that is, the spirit discovers the mockery in which it is living. Then the veil that once obscured its vision of reality breaks, and it awakens to the basic singleness of the being, where everything is one.

According to Buddha, what keeps the Atman attached to the Maya's kaleidoscope, with its uninterrupted transformations and maddening impermanence, is desire. Desire creates attachment, and attachment chains the spirit to sensations, which structures the mirage of shapes and reality of matter.

The Hindu point of view, therefore, is not that of evolutionary growth, but of incessant looping going through diverse and continuous lives, through enlightenment and pain, gradually awakening for what it already is: purity and perfection.

This is the great negative aspect of Hindu philosophies, which discourage any effort of progress, of growth, because the important thing is not to create, develop, but to stop, to get out of the fantasy process of existence, produced by Maya's twists. Hence, the gurus constant meditate – ultimately, meditation is location and immobilism – the cornerstone of individual awakening. The reflection of this negativist philosophy can be seen in India, a country that has been paralyzed for centuries, without the strength to build a more dynamic and creative way of life. That is something that can only be modified at great cost.

The Roustaing Model

The Four Gospels is a mediumistic work received by the medium Mme. Colignon, and J. B. Roustaing, while collaborating. In addition to explanations about the Gospels, purportedly signed *by the Evangelists assisted by the Apostles and Moses (?)*, one is able to find an evolutionary model, which is proposed, for the spirit. According to the reporting entities:

> The spirit is a spiritual essence and is the principle of intelligence from the moment of its formation. It springs from the universal Whole; that is, from the fluids diffused through space, which are the source of everything which exists, either in a spiritual, fluidic, or material condition. The spirit at its origin as a spiritual essence is an intelligent principle formed of the quintessence of the fluids. It is so ethereal that no language could convey any idea of it, especially to your limited intelligence. The will of the Lord God Almighty, the one sole essence of life in infinity and eternity, animates these fluids to give them being by means of a subtle combination, the essence of which is only found in the divine radiance. Thus, he converts them into spiritual essences, which are the primitive principles destined for the formation of the germinating spirit (ROUSTAING, 1971, pp. 108-109).

> When the material worlds are formed, they are composed of all the constituent principles of the different kingdoms of nature which the ages will evolve in the spiritual, material, and fluidic order. The intelligent principle is developed at the same time as matter, and progress with it, passing from inertia to life (ROUSTAING, 1971, pp. 109).

> These multitudinous latent principles remain inert till the Sovereing Master assigns them to appropriate end which they were intended to fulfill under the influence of such surroundings s are fitted to unfold them... (ROUSTAING, 1971, pp. 109).

After numerous transformations, these principles go through the mineral, plant and animal realms, and their in-between shapes, reaching the intermediate state between the animal and the conscious spiritual state. Then, they reach the state of intelligent creatures, who possess Free Will and are responsible for their own actions. But,

It is not known which of the Evangelists or the Apostles (it should not be forgotten that Matthew and John appear in a duplicity of conditions, since they were both Evangelists and Apostles, simultaneously), made such a *revelation*, but wouldn't it be interesting to evoke him to ask whether the spirit's principles, while animating the plant and animal realms, before ego-consciousness, were not *innocent and ignorant*, guided only by instincts? Could they have been guilty and wise? Frankly, I could not understand. Moving forward, it is at this moment that: *The will of the Sovereign Master gives it the knowledge of its faculties, and consequently of its actions; and this knowledge leads to free will, independent and reasonable intelligence, and moral responsibility* (ROUSTAING, 1971, pp. 114).

This means that consciousness is a *gift* God bestowed upon the spirit and not a gradual achievement, due to evolution, as the Spiritist doctrine teaches. Now we have reached the main point of the spirit's evolutionary theory.

Now, let us take a moment for reasoning, starting with some final information. If the spirit abandons the animal instincts, also abandoning its *last animal encasements*, this means that instinctive reflexes can be disposed of without that, therefore, they are not a part of the spiritual structure itself. It is a blatant contradiction with the reality data, especially with Psychology's research.

The comparative study between intelligence and instinct is found in questions 71 to 75, in *The Spirits' Book*, where the Consolidators claim that instinct will always exist in mankind, and it is able to guide them, usually, with more safety than reason. Such instincts are the fruit of the spiritual principle's experiences in the realms of nature, attached to the perispirit, and they are indispensable support to the spiritual existence itself, until the spirit transforms them gradually, by positively directing its own stimulus. In fact, according to the hypothesis under study, it is at this moment that the spirit

The perispirit ceased to be a gradual conquest of the spirit, as André Luiz defends in his book *Evolution in Two Worlds*, to gain the state of *covering* achieved through a *miracle* of the divine, for the criteria for earning is not explained. Now, it is important to ask, how did the spirit, without covering, animate all mineral, plant and animal beings? Would there be any psychic *bonding* connecting it to the bodies it animated? Or was it the *will of God* who kept them in place?

We now come to the first part of the theory in focus. The spirit, at this stage, begins to live in the spiritual world, subordinate to the higher spirits, it will never reincarnate, it will continue evolving quietly in its spirit condition. A blatant contradiction with the Consolidating Spirits' teaching, often reassuring reincarnation as a necessity for all spirits. Reading a little more about this view:

When spirits have acquired the prerogative of free will, and are at liberty to choose for themselves, they are subject to develop their faculties. It is then that their free will leads them to choose one path rather than another. They are more or less obedient to those who are entrusted with their guidance and development, and it is then that they are led to choose a course which may be good or evil. They may fail or may faithfully and gradually pursue the course which is pointed out to them. Many fail but some resist the temptations of pride and envy (ROUSTAING, 1971, pp. 115).

Moving forward, the: *evangelists' spirits, assisted by the apostles and Moses (?)*, demonstrate that they have not evolved in their ways of thinking, not even in erraticity: *Human incarnation is not a necessity, but a punishment...* (Roustaing, 1971, pp. 131).

This is similar to the old theory of *Fallen Angels* but in an evolutionary version. And with some additions, for living through the human body will be longer or shorter, depending on the lasting of previous meekness and the severity of the committed fault, and, just as well, it will dictate the type of World in which it will incarnate, purer and sheerer, or less pure and dense. An interesting fact is that the reasons for falling into the material worlds can be *pride*, *envy* and *atheism* (!).

To conclude, only ruined spirits can reincarnate, because matter is, besides rough, a filthy thing, disturbing, error inducing. The flesh is something putrid, surrounded by miasmas, and the physical world is a place for reprobates, hasty, sinful and revolted spirits. This is a medieval view, which is not consistent with Spiritism. The spiritist and the roustaing model of evolution, despite having some points in common, differ completely and can even be considered antagonists. Spiritism reveals a picture of spiritual growth, from a state of basic simplicity, unformed even, until they reach the complexity of *pure spirits*. The spirits go through a spiritist scale, and some can do it more quickly, if they choose a path of more positive attitudes, with smaller detours, while others prefer a longer track, and park indefinitely on the tracks of moral inferiority. However, all spirits go through reincarnation, where they are subjected to the same tests, before which they have to make their moral choices. There are no privileged spirits in the process. The material worlds reflect the evolutionary state of the spirits that live in them, and progress on an ascending scale, according to the progress of the spiritual group that they host. That is why Spiritism is the comforter, and Allan Kardec could be called the *common sense incarnated*. Just read the following, to check this:

> That is, the guilty spirit who has failed in his earthly experiences is first subjected or tortures corresponding to the faults which he has committed and the to reincarnation, either on your earth or on the inferior planets, according to his degree of guilt, where he is forced by new trials to redeem the past, expiate his offenses, and advance (ROUSTAING, 1971, pp. 198).

And next, a description of how incarnation happens. Falling into primitive worlds, the rebel spirits embody, but not yet in humanoid shapes:

> Such spirits are incarnated in human substances rather than in bodies. The elements of these substances rather than in bodies. The elements of these substances are diffused through space and are afterwards gathered together in the planet where the incarnation is to take place and are combined by the action of the spirits who are prepared for them. Here they are obliged to develop themselves and to progress in the course of successive ages and generations (ROUSTAING, 1971, p. 117).

These *human substances* (whatever this means) are mere sketches, one cannot refer to them as bodies, as read above, but they are rudimentary bodies (!):

> The male and female are neither strong nor developed nor intelligent and can scarcely drag about their gross and shapeless bodies. They live, like animals, on whatever they find suitable for them on the ground. The trees and soil bring forth abundance for the food of every species, and the carnivorous animals do not attack them, for the providence of God watches over the preservation of all (ROUSTAING, 1971, pp. 127).

> They have no instincts but hunger and the necessity of reproduction; but succeeding generations gradually become more developed; their form improves, and they are placed in a dwelling which answers to their increasing requirements (ROUSTAING, 1971, pp. 127).
>
> The spirit becomes to inhabit bodies formed of substances contained in the materials of which the planet is composed; but these elements are so arranged that the spirit can use and appropriate them... (ROUSTAING, 1971, pp. 127-128).
>
> We might better compare them to fleshy fungi; and you may form an idea of the human creation by studying the shapeless larva which live on various plants. Their body forms a nearly inert mass, composed of materials which are still soft and imperfectly combined, and they crawl or rather glide along, for even limbs are almost rudimentary (ROUSTAING, 1971, pp. 127-128).

This is, without a shadow of doubt, something new, whatever that means, we have already been *meaty cryptogamous*. The human being has already crawled through the ground like larvae, so disgusting that the other animals did not feel appetite for it; the problem is that later he became a delicious prey. This is a unique case in the history of Biological Research. Nothing exists in scientific research in the fields of biology, in these last few years to support such conjecture. On the contrary, the evolutionist model has become more and more, a proof of these primitive replicas, until reaching Man, in a continuous biological chain, where the most evolved species emerge from the least evolved. This model has already existed in *The Spirits' Book*, in parallel with Darwin and Wallace's discoveries, founders of the theory of evolution. The great advantage of the Spiritist Doctrine over these products of mediumship is its open system character. In constant exchange with science, without closed points of view, dogmatically established, it is in continuous progress, without becoming attached to spurious and marginal revelations of pseudo-wise or simply mystifying spirits.

The Ubaldi Model

We have seen that, for Spiritism, evolution proceeds from simple to complex, in a clear sequence of increasing complexity. For Pietro Ubaldi, Italian medium, philosopher and mystic, the creation – including the spirit's – takes place in a moment, already done and finished, and spirits would be perfectly generated hierarchy, that is, some higher and some lower, in the sense of subordination. Now, if there is a blatant difference of condition, of hierarchical position, one must ask: what criteria of justice and equity presided over this creation? Why should the spirits thus created, especially those subordinates, submit themselves to such will? Those who were created better than the others, and with greater projection, what did they do to deserve such position? Trying to justify such an unjustifiable posture with a simple: *it was because God so willed*, answers nothing, and it would attribute to Him an authoritarian and partial position, only found in the monstrous being that the Old Testament called Jehovah. Among the spirits discriminated, some rebelled against this Divinity, according to the text, for vanity and pride, thus falling from the energy level, becoming matter, and then initiating a long way back, from the anti-establishment they created to the system, created by God. For a better understanding, we must recall what Ubaldi said in his book *God and Universe*, that by creation we should understand the origin of the perfect spirits, and not our current origin, which is a deformation from the first one. In this first "perfect " creation, creatures were sparks turned into flames due to Love (creation), but remained "One", because they were merged into one unitary organism – God Himself. He then split Himself in order to give the being to the spiritual creatures, but actually split only on his own interior, remaining an organic whole, one and indivisible, of which the creatures, perfect spirits, became a part of. This first creation, purely spiritual, therefore consisted precisely in a transformation of the whole into an organic and hierarchical system, a structural principle that the being tends to repeat, a principle of which he puts us to the test before his own eyes, also demonstrating to us that every being is made in the image and likeness of God. At this point, a new fact comes to light, and it was already described above, because of the misuse that the creature made of its freedom: the angels fell. Part of the spirits rebelled against the system. Our universe is not the creation, but the collapse of Creation, which was spiritual and became material; which was of Infinite character but decayed in the involution of increasingly limited dimensions (UBALDI, 1984, Chap. XX).

As Ubaldi himself acknowledges, there is a resumption of the Fallen Angels theory, in a sophisticated configuration. Such opinion creates great logical obstacles, whose overcoming by Ubaldi leaves much to be desired. What is more, the spirits who rebelled had good reasons for doing so. In fairness, they did not conform to the arbitrarily granted status and rebelled. Happily, from what I have gathered, I suppose I was among the rebels and, if such attitude of the Divinity was true, I would continue rebelling for all eternity.

In fact, the above-mentioned theory is a later invention of Pietro Ubaldi, because the first evolutionary model expressed in *The Great Synthesis* has nothing to do with it. I believe Ubaldi's Catholicism prevailed, and he sought a way to return to terms with the Holy See. Here is a succinct study of the first evolutionary model designed by *Your Voice*, the spirit that psychographed the fundamental book of Ubaldi's collection: the ruined spirits suffer a structural change, and then form the basic principles of matter: atoms. These, in turn, like demonstrated by Mendeleev's table, go through an evolutionary process, which culminates in heavy and unstable atoms that belong to a radioactive series, initiated with Uranium. At this time, matter becomes energy again, going through a new evolutionary stage, which will disembark in the formation of protoforms, or monads, spirituals. The spiritual protoforms then come to animate matter, that is, they will become the spiritual principles of atoms, molecules, of all things. After the stage in the innate world, the primitive psyche continues to animate the primitive biological forms of plants, then turning to animals and acquiring, in the human species, the ego-consciousness and with it the Free Will and responsibility for their actions. From there, evolution will be achieved by the spirits own Volition. Without question, this model is a thousand times more logical and superior to the one Roustaing once provided, although it still maintains the infamous fall of the Angels, transferred now to the beginnings of creation, as it is in the postulates of Christian orthodoxy.

In particular, I lean towards this model, excluding the *prêt-à-porter* creation, with its Marxist Angels fighting against an abstract class system, seeking social equality in the unjust and arbitrary system of an arrogant and partial God. The monism that integrates creation in a single evolutionary process seems very logical. It answers the question of the existence of matter, which is seen as a stage in the construction of the spirit, and not as a separate creation, only to serve one of the other constituent elements of the universe: the intelligent principle.

2. PHYSICS AND SPIRITISM

Overview of the Progress of Physics

Physics is a science that has naturally developed since the early days of humankind due to natural contingency. I mean, of course, empirically. Finding the appropriate solution for the weight ratio and thrust force in hurling projectiles, for the purpose of hunting and feeding. Solving problems related to the relation between force and impact angle, of a rock on top of the other, of a bone or tree branch on top of a stone, to obtain the necessary tools for the work carried out. Identifying suitable ways to build effective and lasting shelters. Identifying materials that could produce fire. Starting the Bronze Age, primitive man had to find more adequate means and ways for building smelting furnaces, establishing the criteria for civil construction and building up megaliths such as dolmens, menhirs, cromlechs and other monuments. And so on. But only in modern times was it possible to discover and enunciate the laws governing the many different phenomena covered by Physics.

In western cultural scene, from the seventeenth century to the end of the nineteenth century, the classical theory was the dominant one, in the domains of Physics. Its patron was the scientist, astrologer and occultist Isaac Newton, who used mathematics to explain the movement of bodies, both in the past and in the future, in a simple and objective way. With few and simple formulas, Newtonian physics describes the laws of movement, applicable to any type of displacement. All of his formulas were developed from a basic equation:

$$d = v. t$$

Where:

d = distance sought;
v = speed with which the mobile moves;
t = time spent on the route.

It is said that, while Newton was watching the moonrise, sitting under an apple tree, an apple fell on his head. After the scare, he began to wonder if the force that made the apple fall, would not be the same that kept the moon spinning around the Earth. Thus, was born the law of Universal Gravitation axiom, which he expressed as: *matter attracts matter, in the direct ratio of masses and inverse of the square of distances*, and which is represented, mathematically, by the following equation:

$$F = G (m.m' / d^2)$$

Where:

G = gravitational constant,
m.m' = masses of the analyzed objects, and
d = distance between them, starting from the center.

The Astrophysical theory of Isaac Newton's time stated that the universe was infinite in time and space. It had been created by God in a given instant, it would exist for millenniums, never-ending. Likewise, it claimed that the universe was infinite in space, that is, to wherever one moved, there would never be a *final frontier* to find. At the end of the twentieth century, after a period in which the theory of a *curved Universe*, that arose from the *theory of relativity*, prevailed, in a closed circle, the chemical observations of microwave irradiation that reaches us, carried out by astrophysicists, direct theoretical thought through the elaboration of the Expanding Flattened Universe, perhaps, infinite; this depends on the quantity of matter and energy in it. Current research points to a "small" volume of visible matter, and an indeterminate volume of *dark matter*. Only with this problem's elucidation one could understand the future of our Universe: a "death" by Infinite distancing from the galaxies or by great compression, due to the force of an inexorable return to primitive singularity, where it all began. It is possible that this return will take place, whether or not the universe is a huge sphere or a huge discoid that is expanding.

Newton's perceptions led to a *scientific world view*. Events should occur according to the *causality principle*, which states that every effect is produced by a cause. This principle was established as an *unquestionable scientific dogma*. Likewise, both space and time were conceptually *absolute*, and its phenomena became instantly interconnected: the flapping of a butterfly's wings in Africa could generate information. For many scientists of the eighteenth century, and most of the nineteenth, space was understood as an extensive linear void, where phenomena occurred at absolute times. The whole theoretical set, however, was about to undergo a radical transformation: new, and equally great, scientific achievements of the nineteenth century.

Parallel to cosmic research, the structure of things was under investigation. The most important and basic deed, in this field, was the resurrection by John Dalton (1766-1844), in 1803, of the intuition about the "atomic" matter structure, proposed by the Greeks of Abdera, Leucippus (fifth century BC) and Democritus (about 460-370 BC). The Greeks also revived the study of magnetism and electricity, which ended up completely modifying human history itself. In fact, it can be said that *atomic theory* and *electromagnetism* triggered a process of *radical mutation* in the historical process; placing humanity on another social-cultural level, transforming the evolutionary rhythm in such a way that only a catastrophe of planetary dimension could revert.

Several scientists, dedicating themselves to the study of *energies* then studied, promoted new and important discoveries. Among these, William Crookes (1832-1919), who did experiments on electric discharges in the vacuum, the cathode Rays, in 1879, concluded that they were electrically charged particles, and affirmed the existence of a new state of matter, which he called *radiant matter*.

On November 8, 1895, Wilhelm Conrad Röntgen (1845-1923), using a *Crookes tube* to study the effects of cathodic Rays' projection on a sheet of paper treated with barium platinocyanide, noticed that it emitted light, with a characteristic brightness. As it happens, there was a dark craft paper in front of the source emitting the Rays, preventing the passage of light rays. After changing the blocking element, using several other materials, he found that none of them were able to intercept cathode emissions. Then, by accident, his hand slipped before the Rays, and he saw that his skin had become transparent, and the bones under it barely appeared. The X-rays were discovered.

Inspired by Röntgen's results, Henri Becquerel (1852-1908) went on to study the relation of x-Rays and fluorescence. In 1896, while experimenting with uranium salt, he casually stored it with photographic plates – which were properly protected -, and the pictures' development showed quite sharp silhouettes, hence the concept of "invisible rays emission" by some substances. The next progress came with the couple Curie [Marie Sklodowska (1867-1934) and Pierre Curie (1859-1906)]: after a series of tests with several elements that emitted energy, using the *Quartz Electrometer* – designed by Pierre –, they verified that the radiance varied between them, becoming clear that the origin was Atomic. Madame Curie proposed, for the phenomenon, the name *radioactivity*.

In the same period, the existence of electrons was proved by Pieter Zeeman (1865-1943), who reached this result by observing the polarization of the edges of spectral lines created by the magnetic field. When communicating his discovery to Lorentz, he sensed that the effect had been produced by charged particles, which had moved within the atom. The name Electron was proposed in 1894 by George Johnstone Stoney (1826-1911).

In 1897, Joseph John Thomson (1856-1940), who was also working with Crooks' vials, proved the corpuscular structure of the cathode rays by measuring them, their velocity and the relation between charge and mass; using Wilson's (Charles Thomson Rees – 1869-1959) condensation method, in 1899, he measured the electron's charge and mass. Thomson proposed the first model for the atom; he imagined it would be a somewhat electrically positive granule, with scattered negative portions through the surface, the electrons. This model became known as Raisin pudding. Later, in 1911, Ernst Rutherford (1871-1937), when working on radioactive emissions, helped by the then student Ernst Marsden (1889-1970), noted that the alpha and beta particles were, on some occasions, deflected, even taking a trajectory opposite to the initial direction. He then concluded that Thomson's atomic model was not correct, but that the atom had a dense, positive nucleus. He then suggested a new model, resembling a planetary system, where the nucleus, electrically positive, was surrounded by electrons, electrically negative, which described orbits around them. However, this model was defective and did not explain why the electrons did not precipitate to the nucleus, as it would be expected. Focusing on the problem, Niels Bohr (1885-1962) attributed fixed orbits to the electrons, stationary states, described by integer positive numbers, where the action and the Planck constant absolutely apply.

In 1900, Max Planck (1858-1947), studying *ultraviolet catastrophe*, explained it by introducing the notion of *quanta*. The *ultraviolet catastrophe* arose from Rayleigh (John William Strutt, 1842-1919) and Jeans' studies (James Hopwood, 1877-1946) on the radiation of black bodies. The calculation of energy's spectrum confined in a blackened cavity produced a result that required high-frequency vibrations to have an infinite amount of energy. It was a blatant contradiction with reality. As Rayleigh and Jeans assumed that energy penetrated and exited a black body in continuous form, Planck, resuming Newton's theory on the corpuscular structure of light, alongside Huygens' (Christian – 1629-1695) Wave Theory imagined the absorption and radiation of energy in the form of discontinuous sets, which he called *quanta*. Albert Einstein (1879-1955) used this solution, in 1905, to explain the photoelectric effect, applying the discontinuous motion of particles concept to light, calling these photon particles, which earned him the Nobel prize. Thus was born the raw material for the Copenhagen School to create quantum theory, with the generalization of its concepts to all atomic particles.

In the same year that he launched his study on photons, Einstein published *The Theory of Special Relativity*, in an attempt to deepen the Vector Theory, which he magnified in 1915, in the theory of general relativity.

With the Theory of Relativity, there was a revolution in the scientific conception of the Universe. Space and time were interrelated discoveries, which formed a continuum that, according to Hermann Minkowski (1864-1909), is a four-dimensional whole. Most importantly, they ceased to be merely abstract notions to become concrete realities, able to be distorted, under the Empire of physical forces. Space bends under the pressure of great masses, proving it to be elastic; while Time, on the other hand, can stretch or shrink, like any material substance.

All bodies, in the same way as space, shrink in size according to the movement to which they are subordinate. As demonstrated in 1913, by the Dutch physicist Hendrik Anton Lorentz (1853-1928).

In 1887, Albert Michelson and Edward Morley were trying to find scientific proof for the existence of ether through an interferometer, mounted on a lead base, which floated in mercury. Ether was considered a substance that filled the spaces, and a mean through which the light waves would propagate, as sound waves propagate through the air. The measurement of the two rays of light that traveled equal routes, from different points, did not present any discrepancy. This contradicted the prevailing belief in Physics at the time.

> Based on the Michelson-Morely experiment, the Irish physicist George Fitzgerald, and the Dutch physicist Hendrich Lorentz, suggested that bodies moving through the ether would contract, and that clocks would slow down. This contraction and slowing down of clocks would be such that people would all measure the same speed for light, no matter how they were moving with respect to the ether. Fitzgerald and Lorentz still regarded ether as a real substance (HAWKING, 2006, pp. 6).

Lorentz is considered by Emílio Segrè (1905-1989), 1959 Nobel Prize in Physics, *a link between Maxwell, Einstein and Planck's generation* (Segrè, 1987, pp. 9).

As stated above, since Newton had launched the proposition of universal gravitation, it had been thought that there was instant communication between objects, so that, if an object fell from a table, at the same time the whole universe would be informed and would suit the new situation. Newton himself was indeed suspicious of this, drawing attention to its physical impossibility. Meditating about this, Einstein concluded it was impossible and abandoned it, imagining that the great masses should cause a distortion in space, as a heavy sphere does, when placed over a stretched net, forming a vortex to which all the surrounding bodies are automatically attracted. This could be verified, as the light should suffer distortion when passing near a star, like our Sun, which would only be possible if space were distorted. This brilliant conclusion was proved by expeditions promoted to verify this thesis, the most forceful feeling that was held in the city of Sobral, in the state of Ceará, Brazil, in 1919, during a solar eclipse. The light deviations noted were 1.61 and 1.98, with an average close to the 1.75 arc seconds calculated by Einstein. Therefore, gravitation is a phenomenon that takes place due to spatial deformation. The planets always dislocate in free fall, in a straight line, but their trajectory has to suit the circular direction, imposed by the distorted space.

The Einsteinian Revolution opened a new perspective for contemporary scientific thought. It enabled the appearance of new theories, which imposed challenges, questions, perplexities and answers to current scientists. We have seen that Einstein was the first to directly question the problem of space and time. Using the studies of the mathematician Georg Friedrich Bernhard Riemann (1826-1866), extended by Ricci and Christoffel in Tensor calculus. Analyzing the problem of movement in his theory of restricted Relativity (1905), the German sage showed us that time cannot be separated from space. Every *event* takes place in the space-time that varies according to the observer's position. In the theory of relativity, time is presented as a pseudo dimension, because the time in which an event happens and is measured must be added to every measurement in space.

The theory of relativity does not state, as it is usual to read and listen, that *everything* is relative, pure and simple. It states that *everything is relative to the Observer.* For example, if two interplanetary travelers, with different locations and speeds, see an event, they will signal different times. Who is right? Both, because the measurement of time will happen according to each one's speed and position, in *relation* to the event.

Time varies from one place to another and according to movement, as can be seen, both in everyday experience and with the use of the formula previously seen, which mathematically expresses the relationship between speed, space and time in uniform motion:

$v = d / t$

From this relation we can get an expression that leads us to discover time, starting from the ratio between distance and speed:

$$t = d / v$$

By varying the speed in an increasing direction, time will logically decrease in the same proportion without, however, achieving a situation of $t = 0$ (even when the speed of light is reached), however fast the dislocation. This decrease in time occurs inside a vehicle that moves at any speed; however, it is of great magnitude when it is quite high. Example: for an observer placed outside an apparatus which moves very quickly and allows the view of a clock placed inside of it the decrease in the course of time will be flagrant, although for the crew everything will remain normal. A comparison between the on-board clock and the Observer's clock will show that the first one was lagged behind the second, which will be more expressive the higher the speed achieved. In addition, time is linked to the velocity of light, which is a universal constant. The more the body approaches 300,000 km/s, the slower time will flow to it, until, once such a speed is reached, it will tend to zero. In other words, time would be frozen. This conclusion is simply theoretical speculation, with no links to reality, as there are no experimental conditions of proof in our Universe. That, however, is not all.

Once the barrier of light has been overcome, time would simply begin to flow in the opposite direction, in other words, there would be a negative growth for whoever would be inside the body. The equation that verifies the dilation of time is as follows:

$$t = T / (1 - (v/c)^2)^{1/2}$$

Where:

t = time elapsed for the Observer;

T = time spent inside the body;

V = body speed, and

c = speed of light in a vacuum.

Such a consequence of The Theory of relativity cannot be proven *in totum*, for the time being, because of a physical impossibility: to reach 300,000 km/s, the body would have to waste more and more energy, for an increasingly smaller gain in speed increasement, as it would absorb ever greater amounts of energy, increasing its mass to Infinity; every moving body undergoes a compression in the direction of motion and, as it approaches the speed of light, would tend to zero volume. However, smaller experiments that used the atomic clock, such as trips to the moon, demonstrated evidence of time decreasement. The Nobel Prize in Physics, Paul Dirac (1902-1984), ventured, in 1928, the existence of a particle that would time travel from the future to the past. It was detected by Anderson, who called it Positron, and Enrico Fermi (1901-1954). Seeking to explain the decay of positron, he imagined the existence of the Neutrino: a particle without mass and electric charge, capable of crossing a lead wall of the solar system's thickness.

In fact, we have talked about the flow of time, when in truth it is debatable because it is not possible to measure that flow. The clock marks time intervals, but not its flows, nor the behavior of that flow. J. W. Dunne, English engineer and mathematician, in his *An Experiment with Time*, in 1927, launched the idea that people wander through time, which would be motionless as space. Dunne became interested because of the premonitory dreams he had had. His study is an attempt to explain the possibility of knowing something that has not yet happened. The question is out in the open and offers a vast field for studies and research. Pietro Ubaldi wrote the saying of the spirit so-called *Your Voice*, concerning:

> Your concept of an absolute space and time, universal, always equal to themselves complies with a purely metaphysical orientation that mathematicians and physicists have unconsciously introduced into their equations. This starting-point, completely arbitrary, has led you to erroneous conclusions; it has placed you before phenomena that vanish into enigmas, before inescapable contradictions and irremediable conflicts, and mystery encircles you on every side. In reality, as I have told, you meet only with a relative time and space, whose value does not surpass the system they concern. But there is more to it. They are only transitory measures in continuous evolutional transformation. (UBALDI, 1959, pp. 145).

Concerning space, these days one speculates with Paul Dirac's hypothesis (1902-1984), that space is not an immense emptiness, but it is structured by virtual atomic particles, which have an ultrashort life, source that creates real particles in certain situations.

The big bang hypothesis or an explosive beginning of our universe, from a primitive condensation of all the existing matter, provides a logical parameter for better understanding the material universe, but it opens a number of questions that experts are looking to answer. It should be noted that this theory is duly substantiated by the results obtained with the measurements related to background radiation, with the Cobe satellite. And today, with the photographs obtained by the Hubble Space Telescope, the knowledge of the cosmos has expanded considerably, almost reaching its border and discovering new and intriguing stellar phenomena.

The question of whether the Universe has a cyclical movement of expansion and concentration remains wide open; if it will expand eternally or if, upon reaching a limit point, it will remain stationary, becoming an immensity of icy, lifeless celestial bodies. It will all depend on the answer to the amount of matter in the universe. I believe, however, as will be seen later, that the theory of the oscillating Universe is the most logical, moving towards the mystical intuitions of the Vedic rishis. Nevertheless, the exhaustive expansion theory is currently in force, with the discovery that galaxies are increasing the escape speed.

Another consequence of the theory of relativity was the postulation of gravitational collapses, as the solutions that, in 1915, Schwartzchild gave to Einstein's equations, which Wheller called *black holes*, due to their ability to retain their own light. The study of these cosmic bodies has been accelerating since 1970 and, everything points that certain phenomena to prove the existence of these *cosmic "cannibals"* have already been detected.

This whole set of knowledge provoked a conceptual revolution, transforming a millennial worldview, as Bertrand Russel pointed out:

> ... is a change in our imaginative picture of the world - a picture which has been handed down from remote, perhaps prehuman, ancestors, and has been learned by each one of us in early childhood. A change in our imagination is always difficult, especially when we are no longer young. The same sort of change was demanded by Copernicus, who taught that the earth is not stationary and the heavens do not revolve about it once a day. To us now there is no difficulty in this idea, because we learned it before our mental habits had become fixed. Einstein's ideas, similarly, will seem easier to generations which grow up with them; but for us a certain effort of imaginative reconstruction is unavoidable (RUSSEL, 1958, pp. 9).

Quantum Mechanics Arises

The studies of Niels Bohr and Max Planck led Louis de Broglie, in 1923, to create wave mechanics, based on the dualistic character of light, in the integers used by Bohr for the electrons' orbits and the analogical agreements between Pierre De Fermat's principle (1601-1665) and Pierre Louis Moreau de Maupertuis' principle (1698-1759). In turn, Werner Heisenberg (1901-1976), in 1925, created Matrix mechanics. In 1926, Erwin

Schrödinger (1887-1961) demonstrated the equivalence of the two mechanics, constructing the matter wave's equation, also known as the material waves' equation, describing the wave behavior of one or more m. mass particles. Quantum physics, unlike classical or relativistic physics, does not produce determined values for future results of an event, starting from an initial value, but from probable values.

The principle of uncertainty is based on the proof that it is not possible to measure, at the same time, the position and the moment of a particle, with absolute precision. For us to observe any subatomic particle, we must throw a beam of light on it, then capturing its reflected radiation. However, when receiving the impact of photons, the particle is thrown back, which affects its moment.

Similarly, there is a principle of time and energy uncertainty, which states that the principle of energy conservation can be violated in very short periods, i.e., energy cannot be accurately determined at a given time at the atomic level. Particles can radiate energy, such as protons, for example, violating, at least in appearance, the conservation of energy, but it must be absorbed in a short space of time, by other particles. This uncertainty principle of the amount of energy in a given time is active in the transmission of forces between intra-atomic particles.

> Heisenberg's uncertainty principle asserts that a similar frantic shifting back and forth of energy and momentum is occurring perpetually in the universe on microscopic distance and time intervals. Even in an empty region of space – inside an empty box, for example – the uncertainty principle says that the energy and momentum are uncertain: they fluctuate between extremes that get larger as the size of the box and the time scale over which it is examined get smaller and smaller. It's as if the region of space inside the box compulsive "borrower" of energy and momentum, constantly extracting "loans" from the universe and subsequently "paying" them back". But what participates in these exchanges in, for instance, a quiet empty region of space? Everything. Literally. Energy (and momentum as well) is the ultimate convertible currency. $E = mc^2$ tells us that energy can be turned into matter and vice versa. Thus if an energy fluctuation is big enough it can momentarily cause, for instance, an electron and its antimatter companion the positron to erupt into existence, even if the region was initially empty! Since this energy must be quickly repaid, these particles will annihilate one another after an instant, relinquishing the energy borrowed in their creation. And the same is true for all of the other forms that energy and momentum can take— other particle eruptions and annihilations, wild electromagnetic-field oscillations, weak and strong force-field fluctuations—quantum-mechanical uncertainty tells us the universe is a teeming, chaotic, frenzied arena on microscopic scales (GREENE, 2010, pp. 119-120).

The *principle of uncertainty* is a law of nature. And it is not based on some deficiency of the appliances used in the studies of the atomic world. Since human bodies are made up of the same atoms that one wants to study, the conclusion is that even the body is formed by particles that behave at random. Finally, the entire universe is composed of particles that can be described as clouds of constantly interrelated probabilities.

It is necessary to radically renew the guiding principles of scientific procedure which, drawn up by Bacon and Descartes, have served as parameter for scientific evolution. The study of the atomic world, placing the mind at the physical borders of our universe, requires a courageous attitude of self-criticism, otherwise, it will remain alienated to mathematical instruments, i.e., to pure mentalism in an exclusive regime. It would be a regression to the Greek position of pure materialism, subordinating the whole process of knowledge to mere mental conceptualizations, distanced from experimental proof.

> This formulation, of course, had unsettling philosophical implications. The Newtonian vision held that the universe was a gigantic clock, wound at the beginning of time and ticking ever since because it obeyed Newton's three law a of motion; this picture of the universe was now replaced by uncertainty and chance. Quantum theory demolished, once and for all, the Newtonian dream of mathematically predicting the motion of all the particles in the universe (KAKU, 1994, pp.115).

The introduction of the *uncertainty principle* in Physics has been generating radical changes in contemporary epistemology since it has been established that the phenomena under observation undergo changes induced by the Observer. Absolute certainty of experimental results was no longer obtained, for they may have happened because the mind of the experimenter led them to that. Observer and observed cease to be isolated elements and became directly interconnected, something which was not conceived in the Exact Sciences, only in the sciences of culture.

Sensory perception, the pride of materialists of all-time *nihil est in intelectum quod non prius fuerit in sensu* (nothing in the intellect has not passed through the senses), ultimately means that atoms and their particles respond to the manifestations of atoms and similar particles. Then an interesting epistemological impasse arises, because observer and observed are one and the same things, causing *axiological neutrality* to disappear – then the scholars of the cultural sciences experimented a sweet revenge –, that the cultists of the exact sciences so much boasted, making us realize that real and complete knowledge of what happens in the atom's world is impossible, except through pure mathematical formulations, but even so with restrictions.

Thanks to the achievements of quantum mechanics, a conceptual revolution is taking place, the implications of which are still being measured by the practical results that it has been providing.

Einstein, who was a causality thinker, was unable to assimilate the consequences of *quantum radicalization*, having spent all his life searching for a unifying theory of the universe's basic forces, which exorcised the probabilistic ghost of Physics, for: "*God does not play the dice*". His quest was a resounding failure, which sidelined him; not only did he fail in the vain effort to combat quantum physics, but this theory has developed so much that, despite numerous riddles and problems that have not yet been solved, it imposes itself on modern electronic pragmatism.

Currently, an intense effort has been developed to find the union between the two physicists, creating a single theory capable of explaining the cosmic and nuclear phenomena. *String theory* seems to accomplish this feat.

Like physics, mediumistic research has undergone a process of growth, as we will see below.

3. THE CREATION

Spiritism and Creationism

Since Spiritist doctrine possesses a philosophical dimension, it studies the principle of things, within an own original metaphysics. It establishes that all that exists has had a beginning, and God is the foundation of all. He created all things. Léon Denis, in his poetic form of writing, stated that the universe offers us the spectacle of an incessant evolution, in which everything has its role. An unchanging principle presides over this work: it is the universal unity, the divine unity, which embraces, interconnects, directs all individualities, all particular activities, making them converge towards a common goal, which is perfection, in the fullness of existence (DENIS, 1977, pp. 148).

Biblical creationism, which supposes a targeted and arbitrary intervention of a hyper-human being, has nothing to do with the *Spirist Creationism*. The Spiritism sees God as a generator and maintainer principle of the universes inhabited by beings and things, whose action proceeds in a natural way, and whose intelligence and wisdom appear in the impeccable logic of the laws governing all phenomena, in all dimensions. Contemporary physics itself already admits, even on an epistemological basis, the possibility of universes parallel to ours, with which we do not have the slightest contact. Spiritism points to the existence of other dimensional levels, with vibratory sub-levels, which are universes in the extension of the term.

> The harmony that governs the forces of the universe reveals certain set combinations and designs, and thus an intelligent power. To attribute the first formation of things to chance would be nonsense because chance is blind and cannot produce intelligent results. An intelligent chance would no longer be chance (KARDEC, 2007, Kardec's comment to question 8).

> Was the universe created or has it existed from all eternity like God? Obviously, the universe did not create itself, and if it has existed from all eternity like God, then it could not be God's work (KARDEC, 2007, question 37).

At the present stage of scientific and cultural development, intending to explain intrinsic mechanisms of creation is not possible because, if one achieves this, they would be equal to God, something that, logically, it is not possible. However, one can speculate on the process of Creation, making analogies from the modern theories concerning the material universe, as well as using propositions of current physicists and astrophysicists.

First of all, it is necessary to establish a number of thoughts on the fundamentals of creation.

The Consolidating spirits refer to a primordial energy, the origin of all that exists: the *universal fluid* (the term *fluid* is due to the mechanistic vocabulary, which became traditional in Spiritism), from which all the constituent elements of the various cosmos derive. Spirits confess total ignorance about the *modus faciendi* (way of doing) of the Divinity when it creates such energy, as one would expect. However, it is necessary to reason that God must be immaterial, posing an initial problem: How can an immaterial source generate a material element? A question that will remain unanswered until the human being reaches an evolutionary condition that allows us to answer it definitively. However, the connection between the immaterial and the material must be gradually made through condensation, provided a type of energy that approaches the generative source's (the Universal fluid) way of being and, by progressive substantial modifications, reaches a state of maximum condensation. While everything that exists must be formed from energy, under modification, this fundamental energy is a logical requirement. That is what we read in *The Spirits' Book*:

> Does matter consist of one or many elements? One single primitive element. The bodies you regard as simple are not true elements, but rather transformations of the one primitive matter (KARDEC, 2007, question 30).
>
> Is the same elementary matter capable of undergoing all possible modifications and acquiring all possible properties? Yes, and this is what you should understand when we say that everything is in everything. Doesn't this theory affirm the opinion of those who do not believe in more than only two essential properties for matter: force and movement, and who believe that all the other properties are only secondary effects that vary according to the intensity of the force and direction of the movement? This opinion is correct, but it should also add: according to the arrangement of the molecules; this may be seen, for example, in an opaque body that becomes transparent and vice versa (KARDEC, 2007, question 33 and its unfolding).

Modern physics has already established that everything is formed from moving energy, organized in accordance with the rules of specific forces. It is also known that there are four organizing forces of matter in our universe: *strong interaction* – which holds the protons and neutrons together inside the nucleus –, the *weak interaction* – which causes the electrons and photons to jump on the radioactive atoms –, *gravity* and *electromagnetism.* Astrophysicists claim that in the primordial explosion, during a minimum period of time, there was a single force, from which those mentioned derived. Einstein spent most of his scientific existence searching for a mathematical formula that expressed this fundamental force and that, therefore, was the universes' own equation. Unfortunately, he was not able to accomplish it. However, he mathematically expressed the spiritist concept of substantial matter and energy unity, with the equation:

$$E = m.c^2$$

Where:

E = resulting energy;
m = mass portion; and
C^2 = the speed of high light squared;

which implies that matter and energy are interchangeable within each other, because, fundamentally, there is only energy, and matter is one of its forms.

We know that all creation exists in God and because of God. Is creation a work that comes from all eternity, or has it started at some specific point? This point introduces the problem of time. If God, an eternal being, created in a particular moment, would have stayed an eternity without anything to do. Being an eternal product, creation would coexist with God, for otherwise it would not be eternal, which would take away its servant status. Co-eternity would necessarily imply its existence in connection with Divinity. Then, there could not have been a creation, considering that everything that exists does not dependent on God, a reality that lives alongside him, as the Greek thinkers had imagined.

Since the hypothesis of the universe's creation in a great explosion arose, the Big Bang, with Georges Lemaitre (1894-1966) and Friedman, deepened by George Gamow (1904-1967), the genesis of time and space was put under the spotlight, until then understood as eternal. According to the hypothesis of the Big Bang, in the beginning, there was a singularity where all universal matter was compressed, including space and, consequently, time. At the time of the explosion, space emerged, expanding until today, due to its elastic feature. Time, by natural consequence, arose at the same instant. Thus, there is no place for the question of what had existed before the creation of the universe, for the non-existence of time would make it superfluous. Nevertheless, if there is no succession of events, how can one establish comparative parameters of meaning? How to reason about the before, if only now and after exist? It would be the same as seeking the knowledge about an extent preceding the zero-point in space. Since time and space are intertwined realities, and the existence of one without the other is impossible, considering they were both simultaneously created, we can only deal with succession and extension from the precise moment in which they began to exist, a situation that, by convention, can be established as a zero instant. Logically, it is only up to us to formulate questions of moment and location, from this point forward, because what is left behind or before has been lost in not being. In addition, as Parmenides established, the non-being is not, only the being is. The Big Bang is the fundamental milestone of existence; the singularity from which it arose was temporal-spatial, unprovided with dimension or successive events, in a monism of the monolithic reality. We can interpret it, and I think we must, as the Parmenian being, that comes from no species.

It should be noted that St. Augustine came to this conclusion already in the fifth century:

> See, I answer him that asketh, "What did God before He made heaven and earth?" I answer not as one is said to have done merrily (eluding the pressure of the question), "He was preparing hell (saith he) for pryers into mysteries. It is one thing to answer enquiries, another to make of enquirers a sport. Seeing then Thou art the Creator of all times, if any time was before Thou madest heaven and earth, why say they that Thou didst forego working? For that very time didst Thou make, nor could times pass by, before Thou madest those times. But if before heaven and earth there was no time, why is it demanded, what Thou then didst? For there was no "then," when there was no time. Nor dost Thou by time, precede time: else shouldest Thou do not precede all times. But Thou precedest all things past, by the sublimity of an ever-present eternity; and surpasses all future because they are future, and when they come, they shall be past; but Thou art the Same, and Thy years fail not (ST. AUGUSTINE, 1999, XI, 12, 14).

Some scientists, such as Ilya Prigogine and Stephen Hawking, argue the existence of an imaginary time, at a right angle to our time. For Prigogine, this time would precede the Big Bang and the creator of this, and the beginning of the universe, which would be a direct product of entropy and not a negentropy process. That is, the creation itself would be the fruit of disorder and not a decay of order.

Current Astrophysics points to an explosive beginning for our universe, collecting lots of data in favor of this theory, since the discovery of galactic escape by Edwin Hubble (1889-1953) at the end of 1920s, until the cosmic background radiation, detected by chance by scientists at Bell Co., Arno Penzias and Robert Wilson. If this universe had a beginning, an estimate of 17 billion years ago made by scholars, it implies that all the other universes had it, too. One may want to place the spiritual universes as permanent, but this leads again to the question of coexistence.

The creative cycle, however, keeps in itself another range of problems. It does not meet the requirement of the first creation; it simply multiplies it in an infinite series of beginnings and endings, falling back on the question of co-eternity.

As we see, the subject is of extreme difficulty, when reasoned in terms of our common experience, with the universe being part of our reality, but not of God's, which is supratemporal and supraspatial. In this case, it really makes no sense wanting to examine something that exists out of time with reasoning and analogies based on it. The creator overlaps and extrapolates creation and is not subordinate to it in any way. *God's intelligence is revealed in God's works, just like an artist's is revealed in his or her paintings; but God's works are no more actually God than the painting is the artist who conceived and painted it* (KARDEC, 2007, Kardec's comment to question 16).

Thus, the separation that the Consolidating spirits make between the creator and the creation is understood, rejecting the pantheism and/or any idea that establishes a substantial causal link between God and creation. The spirit of St. Louis answers with a harsh no to the question about whether the *Universal fluid is an emanation of God* (KARDEC, 2012, par. 74), since the defective verb *to emanate* presupposes a subjective derivation, which would connect each other *physically*, making them intrinsically identical. Interesting to note that Andre Luiz spoke about the Universal fluid, and said that the *cosmic fluid is the divine plasma, the creator's inspiration or His nervous force* (XAVIER, 1985, p. 19), which contradicts the other Luiz, that of France, already quoted.

Deviating from the questions under study, I will be dealing with a philological-grammatical question. There is an interesting expression, used only once by Allan Kardec, in *La Genèse*, chapter XIV, par. 2, but that continues to wander around the pages of some spiritist writers and speakers. I add it here as an interesting fact: *universal cosmic fluid*. As one immediately notices, it is a simple redundancy, a pleonasm. The word *cosmic* derives from the Greek *kosmikos* (cosmic) = relative to *kosmos*, cosmos (World, universe), to the world; thus, the mentioned expression can be transcribed: *fluid relative to the universal Universe*, which is an eccentric way, at the very least, for expressing oneself. The Consolidating spirits created the denomination universal fluid, and, nowadays, cosmic fluid is used by André Luiz, in his *Evolution in two worlds*. The two nomenclatures have the same meaning, that is, a fluid that covers, concerns, the entire universe; one might use one or the other, but never conjugate the two.

The Creation

The question of "how" creation occurs – understood here as a process and not an immediate and definitive fact – faces the same criteria of impossibility. Two great currents debate in this field: the pantheist, which makes God and creation one and the same thing, and creationist, which defines it as extrinsic. I do not argue here materialistic denial simply because it is an inconsistent and illogical fallacy.

Pantheism, instead of clarifying the problem, complicates it. If Creation and God are one and the same, we have abolished the concept of divinity as Creative Intelligence, managing the process of creation, since when He would be the process Himself, and as such, in perpetual change (KARDEC, 2007, questions 14-16). It is a revival of Heraclitian thought, making *movement* the only reality. But, as movement signifies impermanence, God would be the change, but changing is an equivalent to transformation, evolution, that is, constant improvement. Now, a primordial cause in perennial modification could not develop and maintain permanent laws of their own evolutionary coming-to-be. The incoherence does not present itself in the studies of universal phenomena. Not even the most ardent advocate of the current probabilistic view of subatomic phenomena will be able to propose a chaotic structure of the universe, despite the attempts of Neo-Darwinists, regarding the appearance of life and its evolutionary process. Even if matter's "upholstery" presents only an analyzable stochastically elaboration, the macroscopic resultant is decisively and causally ordered, managed by comprehensive and constant laws.

The Aristotelian thesis, in turn, starts from a spatial conjecture: God on one side and creation on the other. But, as it defends the Divine omnipresence, it cannot postulate that something may be exterior to God, for the attribute demands that everything must live within Him.

The spirits who participated in the consolidation did not want to approach the problem of creation in an explicit way, and they did so indirectly:

> Therefore, would there exist two general elements in the universe: matter and spirit?
>
> "Yes, and over everything is God, the Creator and author of all. These three elements comprise the principle of all that exists – they are the universal trinity. However, to the element of matter must be added the universal fluid20, which plays an intermediary role between spirit and matter per se, since matter is too dense for spirit to act upon it directly. Although from a certain point of view this

<blockquote>
fluid may be regarded as part of the material element, it differs from it due to special properties. If it were simply matter, there would be no reason for spirit not to be matter too. It is placed between spirit and matter, yet it is a fluid, just as matter is matter. In its countless combinations with matter, and under the direction of spirit, it is capable of producing an infinite variety of things about which you still know very, very little. By being the agent upon which spirit acts, this universal, primitive or elementary fluid is the principle without which matter would forever remain in a state of dispersion; it would never acquire the properties given to it by gravitation" (KARDEC, 2007, question 27).
</blockquote>

Matter, therefore, is vibrantly placed far away from the Intelligent Principle, to the point that an intermediation of a primary substance, the Universal fluid, is required so that the two elements can interact. But the very sequence of "principles": God, Spirit, Universal fluid and matter, surreptitiously imposes a chain of derivation, in descending order of gradation, which should be supplemented by a positive retrogradation movement to the initial point, i.e., an evolutionary ascension.

The Monistic Solution

After overcoming the traditional materialism, for which matter was the origin and the end of everything, comes the modern materialism, most appropriately denominated as energy. It is a modification of traditional materialism, as a result of the radical conceptual change about the matter, produced by Albert Einstein's Theory of Relativity (1879-1955), which demonstrated that only energy exists, and it constitutes everything, according to its speed and direction. In fact, the concept that matter is coagulated energy is a truth born from the collective unconscious, as can be seen in the following quote:

<blockquote>
… for according to the Vedãntic teaching, matter (prakrti) is materialized energy (prãna, śakti), which, in turn, is the temporal manifestation of that incorporeal, supra-spiritual, eternal essence which is the innermost Self (ãtman) of all things. The Self (ãtman) both evolves the phenomenal realm of matter (prakrti) and simultaneously enters into it under the form of the life-monads, or individual selves (jīvas, puruṣas). In other words, all things, in all their aspects, are but reflexes of that one eternal Self – Ãltman-Brahman – which is in essence beyond all definition, name and form (ZIMMER, 1952, pp. 242).
</blockquote>

In a superficial reading, one could imagine that, in the Consolidation, two distinct principles would have been defined, though in permanent interaction: Spirit and Matter. According to unitary and evolutionary logic that permeates the entire Spiritist Pentateuch, this would be a contradiction, a paradox, because "everything is linked in nature" and there cannot exist two different "chains", since one would always grow, and the other would be in a state of perpetual servitude and immobility. Later we will present our proposal for a solution to this absurd existential dichotomy; we will try to demonstrate that, ontologically, there is only one "being", the spirit (as an intelligent principle), and not two different "beings", as some of Kardec's works could lead to believe.

In the Spirits' Book one can identify the energetic concept, in the following passage, where the universal fluid, or primordial energy from which everything else derives (in anticipation to Einstein), is called primitive matter, by natural adaptation to the physical theories then in force:

> Doesn't this theory affirm the opinion of those who do not believe in more than only two essential properties for matter: force and movement, and who believe that all the other properties are only secondary effects that vary according to the intensity of the force and direction of the movement? This opinion is correct, but it should also add: according to the arrangement of the molecules; this may be seen, for example, in an opaque body that becomes transparent and vice versa (KARDEC, 2007, unfolding question 33).

The scientific postulation of a material monism is not only accepted by the Spiritist doctrine but also supplemented by it, extending to the point of encompassing the spiritual and its dimensions (KARDEC, 2007, questions 17-36). The spirit, evolving through matter, defined as *the tie that enchains the spirit, it is the instrument spirit uses and upon which it simultaneously exerts its action* (KARDEC, 2007, question 22), arises integrated to it, and not only in circumstantial interaction.

A view of existential matter unity is presented in the Consolidation:

> There is an ethereal fluid that fills space and penetrates bodies. This fluid is the ether or primitive cosmic matter, the generator of the universe and beings (KARDEC, A G. 2013, Ch. VI, par. 10).
>
> The primitive cosmic matter contained the material, fluidic and vital elements for all the universes that unroll their magnificence before eternity. It is the fertile mother of all things, the first grandmother, and what is more, the eternal generatrix. This substance from which all the sidereal globes have come has not disappeared; this power is not dead, for it still gives birth incessantly to new creations, and receives incessantly the reconstituted elements of the worlds that have been effaced from the book of eternity (KARDEC, A G. 2013, Ch. VI, par. 17).

But the doctrine goes beyond the material aspect, revealing that the forces acting on matter derive from a fundamental principle:

Consolidation, therefore, anticipates scientific theories of contemporary physics and astrophysics, such as the existence of a primitive force, from which everything else derives, and which existed in the early moments of the "Big Bang". The idea of this primitive explosion can even be intuited from the following passage of the book I am quoting:

...the creative power never contradicts itself, and like all things, the universe was born as an infant. Endowed with the above-referenced laws and the initial impulse inherent to its formation, the primitive cosmic matter gives birth successively to vortices, agglomerations of that diffuse fluid, and accumulations of nebulous matter that were divided and modified ad infinitum to generate diverse centers of simultaneous or successive creations in the incommensurable regions of the expanse (KARDEC, A G. 2013, Ch. VI, par. 15).

In another excerpt, the spirits say that this is how everything is chained, from the primitive atom to the Archangel, who started by the atom (KARDEC, 2007, question 540). It can be questioned that the preposition "by " (*par*, in French) has the sense of "through", which would put the atom in question in the condition of vehicle, persisting the lack of the derivative link between the two elements. Regardless, the whole sentence, as well as the answer here analyzed, proposes the logical chain of all the things in nature, including the spirit, as one of its components. By the way, the interconnected and uninterrupted process of evolution is highlighted in other places of The Spirits' Book; I call one's attention to the answer, which thus begins:

Everything in nature is linked together by ties that you cannot yet perceive, and the most apparently discrepant things have points of contact that humans will never manage to comprehend in their present state... Rest assured that God cannot be self-contradictory and that everything in nature is harmonized through general laws that never deviate from the sublime wisdom of the Creator (KARDEC, 2007, question 604).

In questions 606 to 610, of *The Spirits' Book*, it is explained that a human's soul is a natural evolution of animals and that they absorb the "intelligent principle" of the "Universal intelligent element", which complements the monistic concept existing there, and already seen in question 540.

Therefore, in the basic work of the doctrine, the spirits indirectly propose a monistic view of the creative process. And it could not be in any other way, since the very existence of a Creator, and only one, presupposes a globalized plan of creation, developed and implemented in a uniform manner, where each step contains and matures the next steps, without a solution of continuity.

The point to be discussed in the monist view is not "how" God creates, because there is a lack of conditions for logical thinking that does not allow us to understand the means and way employed by Divinity in the realization of the cosmogenetic process, but the fundamental substance created by Him, from which both matter and spirit derive.

The *spiritist monism* anticipates the Ubaldi monism, explained in the Great Synthesis, in which the author defends the thesis of creation by God and in God, that is, God creates, but from Himself, and not from "nothing", as taught by creationists in general, exception made in the Spiritist doctrine, which peremptorily states that *nothing does not exist*, as Parmenides intended: *The being is, the non-being, is not.*

"Your Voice", the entity that inspired the book cited, draws the creation, briefly:

God ⟶ Matter ⟶ Spirit.

According to this macro *equation of substance*, the spirit is the result of matter's evolution, which, in turn, is an extension of the Divine itself.

The Creation's Essence

Consolidation affirms, as we have seen above, the existence of a primary substance, from which the matter originates in its various aspects: *Universal fluid*. The term *fluid* is a mechanical philosophy's legacy, which in the Spiritist doctrine has acquired its own connotation as an indication of something that precedes *energy*, understood in accordance with the Physics vocabulary. But it does not indicate that the spirit is a derivative of it, quite the contrary, as seen above, in the answer to question 27, the primary substance plays an intermediary role between matter and spirit – I use the word spirit as an *intelligent principle of the Universe* (KARDEC, 2007, question 23), appearing apart from each other, interconnecting only so that one can be *intellectualized* (KARDEC, 2007, question 25). Allan Kardec came to think of naming the spirit as *intelligent matter*, in contrast with the *inert matter* (KARDEC, 2007, question 28), which seems to us to be an understanding of the substantial causality between the two. Or, what I go on to speculate, that the *intelligent principle* could be the primary substance of all substances, including the *universal fluid* itself.

The Creation's Intelligent Principle

It should be clear that we lay our proposition on metaphysical speculation grounds, and not as an affirmation of an unfathomable reality.

We know today, thanks to the Theory of relativity, that matter and energy are interchangeable within each other. Even more, there already are scientists proposing that intelligence manifests itself at all levels of nature, varying only the degree of this manifestation, due to the structure it conveys. This way, from quarks to higher animals, the presence of the spirit would be evidenced by specific behaviors.

Now, taking this thesis further, we can imagine the "intelligent principle" – that Allan Kardec also calls "the Universal intelligent element" (KARDEC, 2007, note to question 76) – as being the essential substance from which everything else is structured, so the "substance's spiritist equation " becomes:

God ⟶ intelligent principle⟶ matter ⟶ Spirit.

What is the basis for such elucubration? One that to us seems essential: the Spiritist doctrine places us in front of two creative processes: that of God, which is characterized by permanence, and that of spiritual entities, with impermanence as its main trait. That is, what Divinity creates necessarily has the character of indestructibility or, using the temporal category, of *Eternity*, while the one of the co-creator spirits is just as limited in time as in space. To clarify: creation takes place outside the space-time continuum, while co-creation is subordinated to it, submitted to its limitations, as André Luiz once said when addressing the subject, stating that the cosmic fluid is the divine plasma, the creator's inspiration or nervous force. In this original substance, at the influx of the Supreme Lord Himself, they operate the Divine Intelligences added to Him, in the process of indescribable Communion, the great Devas of Hindu theology or the Archangels of the interpretation of various religious temples, extracting from this spiritual breath the barns of the energy with which they build the systems of immensity, in service of co-creation in a larger plan, of conformity with God's purposes, the one who makes them guiding agents of the creation. These glorious intelligences take the divine plasma and convert it into cosmic habitats, of multiple expressions, radiant or obscure, gasified or solid, obeying predetermined laws, and these habitats last for millenniums and millenniums, but wear out and transform themselves at last, since the created Spirit can co-create, but only God is the creator of the whole Eternity (XAVIER, 1985, pp. 19-20).

The element that presents a condition of permanence is the spirit itself, both as an *intelligent principle* and as the *individuality of extra-corporal beings* (KARDEC, 2007, question 76).

The spiritist definition of God as *supreme intelligence, the primary cause of all*, and the definition of spirit: "intelligent principle of the universe", establish a connection due to intelligence. Intelligent cause generating an intelligent effect *in His image and likeness*. On top of both propositions, we build our speculation.

For me, higher intelligence would tend to create "a universal intelligent element", from which everything else derives. The "intelligent principle" would thus be the primordial substance, which, through structural modifications, would build all the others, and the substrate of "intelligence" would remain inside of those and rule all the evolutionary process, becoming a part of its becoming, in the search for more and more improved forms, capable of allowing it to express itself in all its fullness.

This way, I understand, one elaborates a *spiritist monism*, logically structured. The spirit would be the beginning, the middle and ending of Creation. All laws would then work within the spirit, for the spirit and because of the spirit, in the structural complex of Creation. It seems to us as if this is a dynamic metaphysical view, that stimulates the individual process of improvement, by the ethical and spiritualizing conclusions it provides. Matter would cease to be the systematic opponent of the spiritual growth process, an obstacle, source of moral miseries, party to the evolutionary becoming, essentially spirit-like, as an entity. Spirit in potency, collaborating with the spirit in action, and dialectically receiving from it the necessary support to update oneself.

It is worth addressing here, even in passing, the problem of the "Fallen Angels" that, both in the Orthodox Christian view and underlying in the Ubaldi concept of system and Anti-system, appears as a concrete primordial reality. Mostly from his book *God and Universe*. Ubaldi proposes that the creation happened instantly and in detail, with all beings and things holding hierarchically defined positions. However, this first creation kept a decay possibility of the harmonic state, which came to happen. Roughly speaking, one is able to criticize the arbitrary imposition of hierarchical levels, considering that its members had done nothing to deserve them, which would indicate a "divine totalitarianism", discretionary and arrogant. The rebellion would have had reason and made sense, justified by the pursuit of equal opportunities, which the unjust creative act had denied the creatures. Instead of the imposed *punishment* of the fall in the *Anti-system*, the rebels should receive the prize for the courage of rebelling against the preferential arrogance of the creator.

Since traditional Christians understand the "fall" as reaching a differentiated and primordial group in the scheme of creation, the "Angels", and not man, would only be the *consenting victims* of the fallen entities. Within Judaism, this notion comes later, and it does not integrate the "creation myth", exposed in Genesis, where the serpent and the woman are indicated as introducers of Evil in the structure elaborated by the divinity. Pietro Ubaldi interprets the *fall* – of few created beings, and not of *Angels* – as the fact that, to God, evolution originates with an earlier involution. The evolutionary cycle would be represented by a parable, with three stages: a *descent* of the being, which would reach its minimum in the matter, where it would then inflect an ascending curve, the period of evolution itself, to return to the system – resigned to its primitive position – totally purified from the self-chosen fall.

In Spiritism we can deduce that the creative process takes place within the general scheme of involution – evolution, not considering the idea of a perfect initial creation, with a portion to "decay" by improper use of free will. This is why, in order for creation to take place, it is necessary to make a "descent" of the "creative wave", in other words, that the creative principle, as a form of energy, gets gradually and unconsciously denser, until it reaches maximum condensation in matter, in order to gradually refine itself, as in an evolutionary movement, until it reaches the initial "purity" vibration, but in a conscious way. So it seems to Vinicius (Pedro Camargo) when he stated that educating is taking from within. Nothing can be taken from where nothing exists. It is possible to develop the powers of the soul because they really exist in the latent state. Evolution results from involution. What rises from the Earth is what has descended from heaven (CAMARGO, 1991, pp. 33).

Similarly, Leon Denis once said that life is nothing more than the evolution of the spirit, in time and space, the only permanent reality. Matter is its lower expression, its changeable form. God is the one excellent being, source of all beings, triple and one, substance, essence and life, in which the whole universe is summed up (DENIS, 1977, pp.14). In the same work, he also stated that universal life has two sides: the involution, or descent of the spirit into matter, by individual creation, and the evolution, or gradual ascension through the chain of existence, towards Divine Unity (DENIS, 1977, pp.15).

Finally, I would like to emphasize again the speculative quality of our proposition. We keep in ourselves the purpose of stimulating enriching discussions, in the marginalized metaphysical context, in the context of spiritist thought. One should not fail to observe that the Consolidator has included at the beginning of Spiritism's fundamental work: The Spirits' Book, the subtitle: Spiritualist philosophy. And, as a philosophy, Spiritism requires the exploration of all fields to find "knowledge without assumptions"; to which it returns the themes subtracted from the expansion of the "pragmatic knowledge", in a perspective of greatness far superior to that of the golden period in which the privileged minds of Tales, Parmenides, Leucippus, Pythagoras, Heraclitus, Socrates, Plato and Aristotle, among others, had shone. Furthermore, some of these thinkers, besides others, actively collaborated with Allan Kardec's task, in the elaboration of the fundamental principles of Spiritist philosophy.

The Creation's Development

What one can observe in the general structure of creation is the energetic character. Everything is made of modified energy, in the vibratory sense. For the Universal fluid to be creation's raw material, it needs to undergo structural modifications in order to give rise to something else. Naturally, its effect should be a vibratory degree denser than its cause, and therefore, resulting in an energetic degradation.

It is clear that the effect will continue to undergo gradual changes, such as its cause, by increasing condensation. It is logical that this degradation will create smaller, more and more compact dimensions. In the Universe, there are clues that will perform as analogies to the way this is done. The most expressive one is the gravitational collapse of a star, phenomenon known as *black hole*. The concept of *black holes* has existed for a long time. In 1784, John Michell (1724-1793) of Cambridge University in England demonstrated that if the mass of a star were large enough, its gravity would cage light itself, making it invisible to our sight. Pierre Simon, Marquis of Laplace (1749-1827), came to the same conclusion, as he wrote in the first two editions of his *The System of the World*'s preface. However, it was the German astronomer Karl Schwartzchild (1873-1916) who found, in 1915, on his deathbed, a solution to Einstein's equations, and concluded that if the gravitational attraction of a body were strong enough, it would contract beyond the proper structure of space.

The term *black hole* was created by John Wheller of Princeton University in 1986. According to the black hole theory, a star with a certain amount of mass can implode when collapsing, under gravity pressure, until it reaches zero size. All its matter compresses into a region of zero volume and infinite density, drastically deforming space in a whirlwind vortex, where time itself is distorted. Then a singularity arises, to which everything is inexorably attracted, including light, thus creating a true black hole in space, a vortex that attracts all the matter around it, crushing it. The theory predicts the possibility of black holes of various sizes, including microscopic ones that would have been formed shortly after the big bang.

The problem is: what happens to ultra-compressed material? According to the Einstein-Rosen bridge theory, it would open a tunnel to another universe. Using this hypothesis, we can carry forward our speculations, projecting on it the Spiritist principles; others propose that they would open passages for our own universe: it is the theory of wormholes. The outputs of the wormholes would form the White holes, with the return of matter, as energy, to the Universe, thus keeping the law of conservation of energy intact.

Why is it that the phenomenon of gravitational collapse could not occur in other universes, of different dimensions? A progressive concentration of energy, causing matter of one dimension to change vibratory pattern, due to the loss of a dimensional characteristic, creating a new universe, a degree lower?

In *The Great Synthesis*, the path of gradual vibratory condensation is expressed in logical terms, in a relativistic point of view, generating a coherent theory of the genesis of universes.

Focusing on the analysis of the material universe's emergence, it is possible to idealize it as follows: the energy of the spiritual universe – called astral by the Theosophists –, who carried on the name given by Paracelsus (1493-1541), suffered an energy concentration in a certain point, probably due to the vibrational collapse of some of its stars, so the implosion then reached its vibrational limits and its energy, in a state of ultra-compression, disappeared in the vibrational limits, transforming its own four-dimensional configuration into three dimensions. This would be the origin of the big bang, which thus falls under deterministic and coherent laws, losing the characteristic of *miraculous fact* that it bears in the set of current knowledge. Its origin would fit into the causality process, and the problem of energy conservation would be solved, as the created universe would maintain a perpetual vibratory exchange with the mother Universe and, as a whole, everything would remain energetically balanced.

Note that the state of energy concentration happens also in our universe, not only in the case of black holes but as well as in the periodic scale of the elements, where it begins with the simple and stable structure of the hydrogen atom, to achieve the radioactive instability of heavy uranium atoms and their related higher condensation, both natural and artificial. The same should, for functional coherence, happen in the several dimensions, undergoing modifications according to each one's physical structure.

In the specific case of the immediately preceding spiritual universe, its physical laws would be very close to those of the material universe, mainly at the boundary levels between the two. The structural constitution would be the center of dissociable atomic particles, proposing physical and biological phenomena similar to those prevailing in the Material universe. The difference would be the extra-dimensional vector, of the immediate spiritual universe. It would generate a different behavior in the composition of structural parameters, allowing immediate responses to mental commands, because the dimension number four would be responsible for opening channels of direct connection with the mind, through which it would process the emission of energetic matrices, whose lines of force would attract the spiritual atomic particles, creating objects, landscapes, locations, or changing the actual shape of the spiritual body.

The morphological configuration of the spiritual environment would therefore instantly suit the mental images, conscious or unconscious, strongly projected upon it. According to the spirits, this is what happens in the habitat where they live. It is said that the perispirit enjoys the Morphometric properties, so much that it reflects, especially in the newly disincarnated, the physical conditions of its last moments on Earth.

4. FORMATION OF SPIRITUAL DIMENSIONS

Dimension Concept

Dimension is defined as a direction in which an extent is measured. Thus, a point is dimensionless because it does not have an extent capable of being measured. But a line segment has one dimension: length; the plane, which is a surface on which one can lay a straight line in numerous directions, has two dimensions: length and width. As for space, it presents three dimensions: length, width and height.

In general, two variables are used to establish any position in space, as it happens with Cartesian coordinates. When you give someone a store address, you say: follow this Street, after passing three blocks, turn on the first transversal on the right. But if it is an office, in some building, you will add: It is on the tenth floor. That is, a spatial coordinate will be added to both flat coordinates. In this case, it works with three variables, which allows geometry to present itself.

Until now, we have only talked about dimensions that varied from zero to three. What about the fourth dimension? At this moment, the subject becomes more complicated. A four-dimensional location would imply other data. Rudy Rucker presents the term *level of reality* (Rucker, 1991) to the address example under study. This way one could supplement the information by saying: when you reach the tenth floor, cross four *levels of reality*. Then, the person should, upon reaching the tenth floor, move through another dimension, the fourth one.

The cited author seeks to clarify the concept of reality levels by an analogy with colors. Suppose that all things possessed color as one more dimensional quality and that only beings or objects of the same color could interact, while those of different colors stumbled on each other without greater problems, even without realizing it. Suppose, also, that people could change their color by simple volition. Thus, upon reaching the tenth floor, the individual would only have to change its color to that of the intended *level of reality*, instantly shifting to it. An interesting fact is that the *reality levels* could co-exist simultaneously in the same space. But in what direction is the vector of the fourth dimension located? To answer the question, we must ratiocinate. Each dimension adds a vector to the immediately preceding dimension, thus creating a new reality that includes the original reality. Exemplifying:

Starting from the point that by definition is dimensionless:

Comes dimension one, which is the line:

By definition, a line is a succession of points (…………). Thus, the dimensionless creates the first Dimension, whose degree of freedom is always one. On the line, a moving point dislocates, moving forward or backward, because the is no other possibility of variation. But this is already a gain since in the previous dimension there was no degree of freedom, that is, moving was impossible.

Now we come to the second dimension, where two or more lines can meet and/or intercept:

The figures featured and all those studied by plane geometry, since Euclid. Length and width combine themselves. Two degrees of freedom are acquired. One body can move, from now on, forward and backward, from one side to the other.

The next step is the incorporation of a spatial dimension: height. The figures acquire the property of volume, as depicted below:

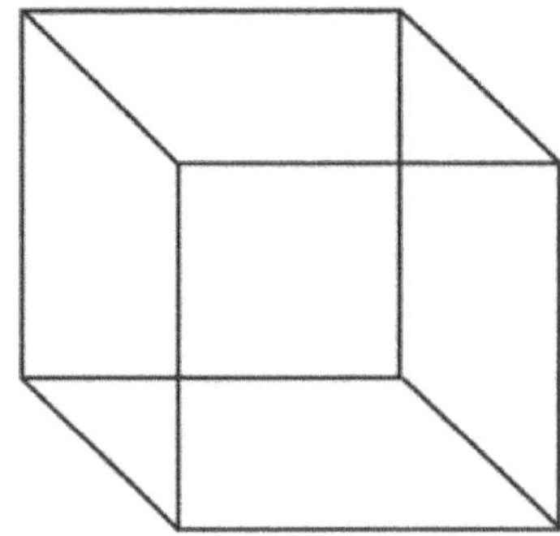

The cube is rather representative of a flat figure of the third dimension. All the shapes studied by Geometry in space fit into this category.

The Fourth Dimension

Now we come to the heart of the problem. How can the Fourth Dimension be represented? What is the meaning of its representative vector? Difficult questions to answer for creatures conditioned by three-dimensional experiences, as Zöllner states:

> In my first treatise, *On Action at a Distance*, I have discussed in detail the truth, first discovered by Kant, later by Gauss and the representatives of the anti-Euclidian geometry, viz., that our present conception of space, familiar to us by habit, has been derived from experience, i.e., from empirical facts by means of the causal principle existing à priori in our intellect. This is particular is to be said of the three dimensions of our present conception of space. If from our childhood phenomena had been of daily occurrence, requiring a space of four or more dimensions for an explanation which should be free from contradiction, i.e., conformable to reason, we should be able to form a conception of space of four or more dimensions. It follows that the real existence of a four-dimensional space can only be decided by experience, i.e., by observation of facts (ZÖLLNER, 1880, pp. 10-11).

The excerpt below depicts what a current physicist says about the problem of a non-existent fourth or else dimensional sensory experience and their intrinsic phenomena:

> Actually, we cannot visualize higher dimensions because of an accident of evolution. Our brains have evolved to handle myriad emergencies in three dimensions. Instantly, without stopping to think, we can recognize and react to a leaping lion or a charging elephant. In fact, those humans who could better visualize objects move, turn, and twist in three dimensions had a distinct survival advantage over those who could not. Unfortunately, there was no selection pressure placed on humans to master motion in four spatial dimensions. Being able to see the fourth spatial dimension certainly did not help someone fend off a charging saber-toothed tiger. Lions and tigers do not lunge at us through the fourth dimensions (KAKU, 1995, pp. 11).

There is no current experience with fourth-dimensional phenomena that would allow mathematics to calculate bodies of N dimensions, working with equations of N variables, as stated the German physicist and spirits researcher, pioneer of the superstring theory in North America. My purpose, however, exhausts itself in some considerations about dimension number four.

Charles Hinton, studying the subject, suggested the terms *ana* and *kata* as names for the fourth vector, which would raise our third dimension by another degree. With these terminologies, he then thought about how to explain the way a spirit manages to transport an object from one closed box to another in identical conditions. One could say: *the spiritual entity moved the object in the ana direction in the fourth dimension, removing it from the three-dimensional space where it was, and then shifted it in the Kata direction, returning it, now at the targeted location, to the three-dimensional space.*

This, however, is only an expression of what is totally unknown, for one continues to ignore the essential: the exact direction of *ana* and *kata*. They must be quite similar to *up* and *down* or its equivalents, but in what way?

It is possible to make the two-dimensional projection of a four-dimensional geometric figure, as in the case of the Tesseract or Hypercube, geometric shape equivalent to the three-dimensional cube, in the four-dimensional space.

Ratiocinating: the fourth dimension should present similarities with the previous dimensions, i.e.: the first dimension maintains the point while enlarging itself with the line; the second, has the point, the line of compression and then adds width to it; the third incorporates the previous dimensions, incorporating height. Analyzing the three-dimensional phenomena, it is found that they mean the use of previous contributions. The fourth dimension, by its turn, adds to its own vector all the precedents. Therefore, there will be first, second and third-dimensional phenomena. It has already been seen that human beings' movements take place in a dimension in which there are almost two degrees of freedom. Naturally, beings of the fourth dimension will be able to move in a three-dimensional system: in other words, they can move back and forth, from one side to the other and up or down. That is to say, they can float. This points us to the reason corroborating the mediumistic facts, showing the spirits' ability to move, fly, through space. They can walk, which ensures them two degrees of freedom, but the ability to go up and down allows them three degrees of the same freedom.

The stereoscopic view of spiritual beings derives from the fact that they receive three-dimensional images, just as in the third dimension people receive them in two-dimensional ones; but just as one can, through the brain structure, decode light and shadow, in order to have a spatial capture, in perspective, the spirits have enlarged sensations, by the senses of *ana* and *kata*, that is, the four-dimensional vector that, besides the three-dimensional perspective, leads them to perceive around the objects of their world, as if they see them from all sides simultaneously (see Chapter VII, *Mediumship and Evolution*).

Returning to the hypercube, it is, for four-dimensional beings, what the cube represents for three-dimensional beings. Similarly, what in the third dimension is a square, for them is the cube; the circle is perceived as sphere and the sphere as the Hypersphere, the Triangle as a pyramid, etc.

It is possible to represent, in a naturally schematic form, the tetracube, as in the picture below:

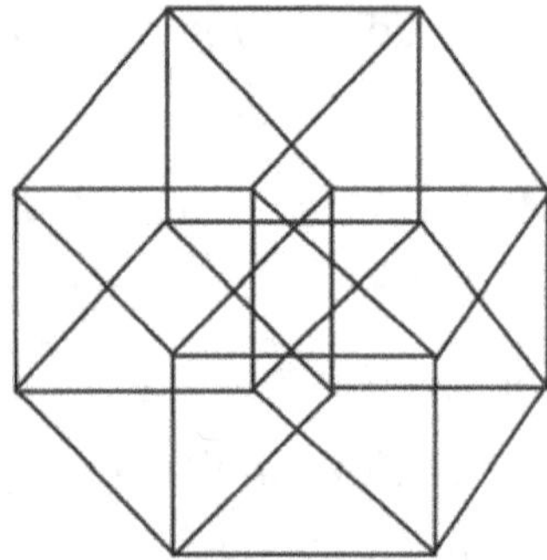

In the illustration, one cannot identify the four-dimensional vector, which distorts the figure that, a pale sample of its own reality. Immanuel Kant was, as far as it is known, the first to address the fourth-dimension subject, relating it to the spiritual world:

> If it is possible that there be developments of other dimensions in space, it is also very probable that God has somewhere produced them. For His works have all the grandeur and variety that can possibly be comprised. In the foregoing I have shown that several worlds, taken in a metaphysical sense, might exist together, but, at the same time, here is the condition, which, according to my belief, is the only one which makes it probable that several such world really exist (ZÖLLNER, 1880, p. 11-12).

Reassuring even more his thought, says the philosopher of Könisgsberg:

> I confess I am much inclined to assert the existence of immaterial beings in this world, and to class my soul itself in the category of the beings. We can imagine the possibility of the existence of immaterial beings without the fear of being refuted, though, at the same time, without the hope of being able to demonstrate their existence by reason. Such spiritual beings would exist in space, and the latter not with-standing would remain penetrable for material beings, because their presence would imply an acting power in space, but not a filling of it, i.e., a resistance causing solidity. It is, therefore, as good as demonstrated, or it could easily be proved, if we were to enter into it at some length; or, better still, it will be proved in the future -- I do not know where and when -- that also in this life the

> human soul stands in an indissoluble communion with all the immaterial beings of the spiritual world; that it produces effects in them, and in exchange receives impressions from them, without, however, becoming humanly conscious of them, so long as all stands well. It would be a blessing if such a systematic constitution of the spiritual world, as conceived by us, had not merely to be inferred from the - too hypothetical - conception of the spiritual nature generally, but would be inferred, or at least conjectured, as probable from some real and generally acknowledged observation (ZÖLLNER, 1880, pp. 32)

These passages were also used by Carl Gustav Jung, in a lecture he gave at the Zofingia student fraternity, at the University of Bern in May 1897, in which he affirmed the existence of the spiritual world and the immortality of the Soul (see JUNG, 1983, par. 77-81). Kant disembodied in 1804, when Hippolyte Leon Denizard Rivail was born, the future Allan Kardec, the one who accomplished the realization of the German philosopher genius' metaphysical elucubrations.

Dr. Friedrich Zöllner, in his *Scientific Treatises,* which I quoted earlier, carried out experiments on the physical effects with the English medium Henry Slade, in which he obtained evidence of the interpenetration of matter by matter, which could only happen via a fourth dimension. For example, sealed and fastened knots on a rope. Whole wooden rings, i.e., without bandages, threaded into the central support of a three-foot table, the top of which was screwed and the fitting with the single piece of the feet solidly fastened, etc. These facts have long been witnessed and achieved in strict conditions of control, since 1848, to the tens of thousands.

I agree with him about the four-dimensional configuration of the spiritual plane that surrounds us. Its inhabitants, therefore, enjoy faculties and capabilities, seemingly miraculous, but which are not, as they are using the natural qualities of the environment, where they live. For a two-dimensional being, the acts produced in its environment by a three-dimensional space being are fantastic, miraculous, a derogation from that environment's laws of nature.

What I have been saying makes clear that, by using the directions *ana* and *kata*, the spirits can perform Spiritism phenomena considered physically impossible, such as: seeing the inside of the human body, diagnosing diseases, being in several places simultaneously, seeing what happens in these distant places, etc., but none of this configures the wonderful or the supernatural.

Current Physics and Dimensions

The material universe, as seen earlier, has three dimensions: forward-backward, sideways, up-down. Einstein, in his theory of Relativity, presents time as a fourth dimension to be added to the existing three. When, for example, a body is located on the surface of the Earth, such as an airplane, one says it is at as many degrees of longitude and latitude, north, ten thousand meters above sea level, at 14 hours, Brazilia Time. The exact position could not be obtained without the time variable, as the aircraft is not stationary. This Fourth Dimension, like the physicist himself had recognized, is a pseudo dimension, acting as one more auxiliary variable, because it does not add more meaning to the extension. In fact, time is connected to space, thus forming the so-called continuous space-time.

But in 1919 Theodor Kaluza suggested that the Universe could have more than three dimensions, based on the theory of relativity:

> In a paper he sent to Einstein in 1919, Kaluza made an astounding suggestion. He proposed that the spatial fabric of the universe might possess more than the three dimensions. The motivation for this radical thesis, as we will discuss shortly, was Kaluza's realization that it provided an elegant and compelling framework for weaving together Einstein's general relativity and Maxwell's electromagnetic theory into a single, unified conceptual framework. But, more immediately, how can this proposal be squared with the apparent fact that we see precisely three spatial dimensions? The answer, implicit in Kaluza's work and subsequently made explicit and refined by the Swedish mathematician Oscar Klein in 1926, is that the spatial fabric of our universe may have both extend and curled-up dimensions (GREENE, 1999, pp. 187-188).

The Kaluza-Klein formulation added new equations to Einstein's ones, and had an unexpected result:

> Before Kaluza's suggestion, gravity and electromagnetism were thought of as two unrelated forces… Kaluza suggested that there was a deep connection indeed. His theory argued that both gravity and electromagnetism are associated with ripples in the fabric of space. Gravity is carried by ripples in the familiar three space dimensions, while electromagnetism is carried by ripples involving the new, curled-up dimension (GREENE, 2001, pp. 197).

Kaluza's theory contradicted the experimental data. When he sought to incorporate the electron into the theory, there was a discrepancy in the relationships between its load and its mass, which differed from the values known until then. This has led to the marginalization of the theory until the 1970s. Since then, with the progress of the compatibility between some aspects of quantum theory with the theory of relativity, in order to provide a better understanding of subatomic phenomena, such as in the formation of *relativistic quantum field theory*. Which is:

It's quantum because all of the probabilistic and uncertainty issued are incorporated from the outset; it's a field theory because imerges the quantum principles into the previous classical notion of a force field - in this case, Maxwell's electromagnetic field. And finally, it's relativistic because special relativity is also incorporated from the outset (GREENE, 1999, pp.121).

Today the string theory is the one in development and appears to show possibilities of unifying both physics. This theory aims to solve the question of particles multiplicity found in nature. A string is an element 100 billion and billions of times smaller than a proton. Each particle would ultimately be the result of a specific vibration of the basic "strings": *The string is so incredibly tiny that, from a distance, a resonance of a string and a particle are indistinguishable. Only when we somehow magnify the particle can we see that is it not a point at all, but a mode of a vibrating string* (KAKU, 1994, pp.153).

The interesting thing with string theory is that it is only defined in ten and twenty-six dimensions: *...the central characteristic of the theory is the geometry of higher dimensions* (KAKU, 2000, pp. 192). That is, what it looked like before science fiction started to become something serious in the realm of Physics. Although Jean Charron said that physics is the one that will prove, beyond any doubt, the existence of the spirit. The more thought one puts into the solution of the substantial problems related to the matter, the more the boundary between the physical and the spiritual diminishes. Next, I will begin to develop the cosmological concepts that were inspired by the spirit of Leonardo Da Vinci.

The Dimensional Universes

Science is gradually overcoming the circular thought of *causes-effects-causes*... Spiritism, upon discovering the *spiritual world*, added new elements, with which scientific thought will have to deal in order to solve the basic problems of contemporary science, that, without it, is lost in an endless sea of insoluble tautologies. On the other hand, it raises new challenges by broadening the field of research and experimentation. This is because the central point of the *Spiritist Revolution* is to prove, beyond any reasonable doubt, the existence and survival of the spirit. This led to the discovery of the *spiritual world*, the natural *habitat* of disembodied spirits, with their structures and phenomena, laws and existential requirements. Consequently, the problem of the spirit's organic

Constitution arose, with the consequent discovery of the perispirit, or *spiritual body*, an instrument that the Spirit uses to exist in its natural environment.

The finding of the *Agglutination law by spirits' Moral affinity*, without a physical body, led to the problem of spiritual worlds' stratification in various vibratory or dimensional levels, a direct result of *perispiritual density*, resulting from a greater or smaller assimilation of telluric energy, as well as strong mental connection with biophysical phenomena, in pathological regime. Clarifying: do not confuse *dimension* with *vibrating levels* or *tracks*.

The dimension is composed of numerous vibratory bands, where the entities of the same dimension are apart from each other due to vibrational nuances, or small variations in frequency. Roughly speaking, such entities belong to the same dimension because they have not yet achieved the psychic harmonization necessary to access a higher dimension. Basically, they still have some negative resemblance in the moral sphere, hence, they are linked to erraticity. The concept of a *Spiritual plane* composed of differentiated *vibratory levels* is sometimes sought to counteract the idea of dimensions. I do not see, in this theory, a denial of the multiple spiritual dimensions, on the contrary, they are conjugated and combined. From spiritual reports, one can deduce there are vibratory levels, in which spirits of the same dimension can coexist in the same place without being able to see or feel each other, due to the different vibratory patterns, one with a higher and the other with a lower vibrational frequency. Likewise, the change of mental frequency pattern necessarily implies in changing vibratory range, meaning a change of Environment, as seen in the example of André Luiz, who, while disturbed by psychic dysfunctions taken from the physical world, after death, remained unable to identify the presence of Clarêncio, who was always visiting him, waiting for the opportunity to rescue him (XAVIER, 1988, Ch. 2). However, at the moment that he raised his vibratory pattern in a prayer, he saw him and the auxiliaries who accompanied him. The environment itself had changed before his eyes, disappearing the foggy region, to give way to another, lighter, illuminated by the sun. He came out of the lower level where he was, instantly passing to an immediately higher level, because of the new psychological position taken. It is a matter of *Affinity law* enforcement. Thus, a dimension can contain a vast range of *vibratory levels* or *Reality levels*.

The translation of a vibratory level to another requires an interference in the type of waves emitted by the mind. If a spirit at a higher level wishes to descend to a lower level, it must assimilate the vibratory pattern of the level, if it wants to be noticed. The vibratory pattern must condense the spiritual body, saturating it with the energies of the band to which it wants to be (see XAVIER, 1987, Chapter IV). The change of dimension bears some similarity, but it is much more radical since it requires the loss of a manifestation vehicle in the case of transfer to a higher dimension, or the acquisition of a vehicle of expression, temporary or long-lasting. This is the case of disincarnation and Incarnation. André Luiz refers to the process when he says it is necessary, in order to achieve a higher plane, or dimensions, to lose the *psychosoma*, or *astral body*, the outermost part of the perispirit that the spirits use to act in the immediate *spiritual universe*. The author himself said that he had accompanied several friends in the reincarnation task when attracted by imperatives of evolution and redemption. Other times, rarely, incidentally, he had had news of friends who lost the perispiritual vehicle, achieving higher planes (XAVIER, 1985, pp. 85).

I think it is necessary to switch the word perispirit to spiritual body, or psychosoma, as André Luiz did in Evolution in Two Worlds, because, as I will try to demonstrate later, the perispirit is not a whole in itself, but a complex formed of energy tracks in a regime of vibrational graduality.

Analyzing the dimensions of the spiritual world in more detail, one can verify that they are real *universes*, where there are galaxies, stars and planets, within the *physical* conditions of each of them. All this is still within the scope of speculative thinking, requiring expert proof, but scientific speculation is a valuable exercise, the genetic nucleus of significant discoveries. Nevertheless, any speculation, to be positive, must be accompanied by already proven facts. It must be a logical unfolding of what is already known, but without requiring a firm commitment to the current reality, to become fertile grant to studies and experiments, analyses and discoveries. Since Thales of Miletus (640-546 BC), speculative thinking has been the matrix of humanity's cultural and scientific growth. The spirit Your Voice, through Pietro Ubaldi, conveyed:

> If your universe is finite as a sidereal vortex, the system of universes, and the system of system of universes is infinite. If space were infinite, it would not have limits in its quality of space; however, it has them, but you will find them not in space, in spatial direction, but in evolutional direction. From this concept, to which we have already alluded, we come now to a very new conception: the only limits to space are hyperspatial, that is, they can be found toward the development of the evolutional march, and precisely in the successive dimension. Better still, if you wish to set a limit to space, you will find it only in its preceding or succeeding dimensions (UBALDI, 1959, pp. 156).

Returning to the matter of *Dimensional Universes*, we can express each universe as the sum of physical (real and virtual), spiritual and mixed (physical and spiritual) entities it contains. As physical entities, I understand the set of primary particles, forces, physical and biological elements that constitute the basic structure of the considered universe; as spiritual entities, the reunion of incarnated and disincarnated spirits as well as spiritual monads and specific energies that belong to it; and mixed to the elements which take part in both natures. In a simple mathematical formulation, one can express each spiritual universe, through a simplistic two-dimensional approach, for analog effect, as it follows:

$$K = \sum_{i=1}^{n} f_i + \sum_{i=1} e_i + \sum_{i=1} m_i \qquad (I)$$

Or

$$K = \sum_{i=1}^{n} (f_i + e_i + m_i) \qquad (II)$$

Where:

K = the universe in its entirety.

f = physical entities;

e = spiritual entities;

m = mixed entities.

n = an immeasurable number.

Note: *Entity has the sense of all things of the universe considered.*

In the same way, the set of universes would be:

forma o conjunto de universos seria:

$$C = \sum_{J=1}^{N} \left(\sum_{i=1}^{n} (f_i + e_{i+} m_i) \right)_j \qquad (III)$$

Where:

C = set of universes.

N = the last considered universe.

Such a set would express the creation itself, and its mathematical formulation can also be written from (II) thus:

$$C = \sum_{j=1}^{N} K_j. \qquad\qquad (IV)$$

Note that I portray the universal series as finite. To make it infinite, just make **j** equal to minus infinite and **N** equals plus Infinity.

Using the nomenclature of the set theory, it can be said that:

F = {physical entities}

E = {spiritual entities}

M = {mixed entities}

So:

$$M = F \cap E$$

$$K = K \cup E$$

$$C = \{K\}$$

The word creation is put purposefully because Spiritism assumes the existence of a *Superior intelligence, primary cause of all things* (KARDEC, 2007, question 1). In other words, God is a fundamental reality in the spiritist conception. His existence arises as a *petitio principii*, from the observation of nature, as well as from all scientific and philosophical reasons.

Morphology of Universes

The morphology of the existing universes must, in all probability, tend to a sphere of finite radius, expanding, without having certain boundaries and concluding.

Each dimensional universe generates what is immediately inferior to it and, in turn, is formed by what is previous to it.

A universe, in addition to creating, exerts on its consequent a constant pressure both from within and from the outside, both physical and psychological, since it envelops and permeates it.

The spiritual universe immediately preceding our own, encompasses it and exerts constant and systematic pressure on it, both in the psychic and in the physical plane, in a double sense: from the inside to the outside, and from the outside to the inside.

Physically, the boundary between the two states of being of matter is an effervescent whirlwind of particles transitioning from virtuality to reality, as Paul Dirac wants, in a constant exchange of dimensional situation, under the pressure of powerful forces. At the same time, the border should behave as a strip where the physical laws of the two ways of being mix, forming a region of peculiar phenomena, where the mixing of unique effects produces singular effects. Theosophists call this interdimensional space the *etheric plane*, which one could see as the generator of life's maintainable energy, called *vital fluid: what is the cause of the animalization of matter? Its union with the vital principle* (KARDEC, 2007, question 62). This intermediate region could be called hyperspace, and it would be fundamentally important in psychic and mediumistic phenomena in general, as will be seen later.

This pantachic boundary between two dimensions should provide the same effects, including vital ones, whichever the dimension considered. The term pantachic comes from the Greek pantakou, and means: in all parts, absolutely. Leonardo Da Vinci's spirit inspired this neologism into me, in order to indicate that the boundary between the two universes lies, between us, everywhere, both inside and outside.

The actions and reactions of electromagnetic fields, as well as other forces, at dimensional boundaries, can have the vital energy (vital fluid) as a byproduct, as well as its correlates (magnetic energy, prana, kundalini, etc.):

> Does the vital principle reside in any one of the bodies known to us? Its source is in the universal fluid; it is what you call the magnetic fluid or the animalized electric fluid – an intermediary; the link between spirit and matter (KARDEC, 2007, question 65).

These reasons about the physical dimension and the spiritual dimension immediately preceding are valid for the relation between a dimension and the one it has had its origin in.

Each universe will have its specific gravity which, naturally, through its polydimensional properties, acts on the lower universes, but with greater intensity about its derivative. This progressive chain of gravitational pressures multiplies along with its progress, by the sum of the gravitational pressure proper to a given universe, with those that dimensionally precede it.

Mathematically one could express the gravitational pressure suffered by a universe as:

$$P = G_n + G_{n-1} \qquad \text{(V)}$$

Where:

G_n = gravity of the generator universe;

G_{n-1} = gravity of the generated universe

The total set of pressures would be expressed:

$$P_t = mG_k + (m-1)G_{k-1} + \ldots + (m-k+1)G_k \qquad \text{(VI)}$$

P = total pressure of the generator universe

m = total mass of the universe

This set of increasing pressures leads us to two considerations:

a) The Shape of the universes should tend to that of a sphere, which is the pattern found in all cosmic phenomena, both in the whole and in the singular. It must represent a sphere of finite radius, although incommensurable by our current standards, lacking determined and conclusive Borders. Thus, Formula IV could be written as:

$$C = (4/3)\, \Pi \cdot \sum_{i=-n}^{1} r\,3 \qquad \text{(VII)}$$

b) the whole will tend to regress to an initial point in a process of gradual resorption when the concentric gravitational pressure overcomes the eccentric force of the set's expansion. Currently, there already exists a hypothesis that proposes a discoid shape for the Three-dimensional universe, as the galaxies have, in general. In this case, the above formula should be changed, but the idea regarding the characteristic systole and diastole of the universe's life and death would remain.

The above considerations should be much more complex if one starts from the propositions of relativistic physics that the three-dimensional universe is the outer part of a

Hypersphere, that is, a tetra dimensional sphere. Thus, one would have to work with the concept that the likely sphere, which comprehends all other *spheres-universes*, is a sphere of dimension N, The Shape of which is incomprehensible, rationally.

The cosmos would then have the shape of a four-dimensional sphere, wrapped by another in a fifth-dimensional spherical shape, and so on, up to the set sphere, of Dimension N, where cosmos of dimension N-I exists.

I prefer, however, working with simpler figures and concepts, in order to be understood by the largest number of people.

Evolution of Cosmic Systems

As seen, I refer to cosmic systems as dimensional universes that exist, in the process of involving and pervasive integration. Although I have already explained the subject, in detail, in the previous items, I will try to summarize it.

Pietro Ubaldi, whose psychic sensitivity has bequeathed us so much wisdom, in his mediumistic work the great synthesis, places the existence of universes clearly and conceptually logically. His view of energy condensation by the dynamic condensation has found justification, as analyzed, in the most recent formulations on Black Holes, which ultimately represent, gravitational swirling bikes that compress a stellar mass until it disappears from a universe. According to the conception of Einstein-Rosen, this compression opens a throat, a wormhole, a tunnel in space-time, between universes or more distant regions of the universe itself.

Here we return to the ubaldi axioms: the successive evolution of universes that unfold along a path of dimensional degradation.

In my view, such universes are born in a vast movement of systole and creative diastole, which philosophers called: Days and nights of Brahman, or God's breathing movements, where the expiration translates the moment of creation and expansion, and the inspiration the reflux process, return to the divine fulcrum. It is clear that the picture is only a poetic analogy, but it expresses the concept of a creation by birth cycles, development, maturity, old age and death, with periods of stability in the waiting intervals.

Adopting this scheme, I conceive the creative process unfolding in a singular design in which the universes derive from each other, in a system of progressive and constant energy degradation, with retroactive spontaneous flow, when a maximum of dimensional relaxation is reached. The fundamental mechanism of the system would be the punctual dynamic concentration, just like the gravitational collapse phenomena, generator of the black hole, in the considered cosmos. At the point of maximum energy concentration, there would be an explosion in the sense of a lower dimension. In other words, the singularity in a dimension U_n would have as its necessary counterpart a big bang generator from another U_{n-1} universe with the loss of a dimension.

If the problem is applied to the three-dimensional universe, then we will have a Four-Dimensional spiritual universe, suffering a gravitational collapse at any point, which generated the creative explosion of our Material, three-dimensional universe. With this model, we answer the question about what there was before the Big Bang: another universe, which is the origin of the later Born Universe. Another question that finds an answer is the one that asks what will happen to the universe in which humans live. Since it came to exist due to a more comprehensive universe, which involves and permeates the second, it becomes clear that the second universe undergoes constant physical pressure on the entire interdimensional pantachic border, which will lead, over time, to a kinetic reflux, a return to the point of origin, triggering a resorption in the mother Universe.

Another consequence would be that being the occurrence of gravitational collapses relatively common on a cosmic scale, there can be an infinite number of parallel universes, of which there is not the smallest knowledge, or possibility to come to know, physically. In these sibling universes, the most diverse structural and formal procedures of evolution, as well as substantial phenomena, within the organizing criteria escape the mind completely, to the cover-city of imagination.

Extrapolating these speculations to the countless (infinite?) dimensional universes, there would be a huge set of derived universes at each level, therefore unraveling a view of the power and grandeur of the genetic fulcrum-maintainer of the immeasurable process of creation, called God, whom Jesus, in a blaze of tenderness, called Father.

5. ECTOPLASM: SOME OBSERVATIONS

Concept, Composition and Usefulness

Ectoplasm, from the Greek verb *plássou* (to model, to portray, to look like), is a word created by Charles Richet (1850-1935), as he states in his *A Treatise on Metapsychics*. He designates a substance that emanates from the mediumistic organism in trance and is responsible for producing physical effects. It usually has an amorphous condition and presents reptilian or amoeboid movements. It is unstable because it appears and disappears very easily, especially in the face of substances or actions that pose a threat. Its colors range from gray to milky white and may have, on some occasions, a whitish-green hue. It is photophobic before unexpected exposure to white light, even if its intensity is that of a full moonlight. Whenever suddenly subdued to light or unexpected stimulus, it causes a violent organic reaction, of unpredictable consequences, in the medium.

Spirits made references to this substance and its functions, as one can see in the works of Swedenborg, Andrew Jackson Davis and the pneumatographies received at Jonathan Koons's mediumistic Laboratory in 1850 in the United States (see ARGOLLO, 1994). One can define Ectoplasm as an entropic biological state, produced at the expense of the medium's Psychosomatics negentropy: it is the physical body and the biome of the medium in a state of physical disorganization. Proof of this resides within the experiences in which, as the medium's body of dilutes, losing consistency and many times disappearing partially or totally, the ectoplasmic cloud gains greater consistency, producing more intense phenomena.

André Luiz once described it as being the substance, characterized by a special smell, which we could not describe, and that dripped in reptilian movements, accumulating in the lower part of the mediumistic organism, where it presented the appearance of great protoplasmic mass, living and trembling (XAVIER, 1970, p. 235). In all the vital phenomena of nature, ectoplasm is an indispensable element. André Luiz also asserted that the perispiritic matter, just as a product of the soul's emanations thought the filter called body, is resource peculiar not only to man but to all forms of nature (XAVIER, 1970, p. 244).

And further on, in the same work, he mentioned that these rays (ectoplasmic) are peculiar to all living things. And with them, the caterpillar performs its complicated demonstrations of metamorphosis and it is still on their basis that all the processes of mediumistic materialization are carried out, because the embodied sensitives that favor them, release these energies more easily. All creatures, however, keep them within, emitting them in variable frequencies, in accordance with the tasks that the plan of Life points out to them (XAVIER, 1970, p. 24).

In mediumistic meetings, in general, ectoplasm is used for the most diverse purposes, as we read in "Missionaries of light", of the same author. He stated that each member of the mediumistic meeting then studied by him, emitted light rays, very different from each other, in intensity and color. These rays were confused at a distance of approximately sixty meters from the physical bodies and would then establish a current of force, quite diverse from the energies of our sphere. This current was not limited to the moving circle. At a certain point, it poured out vital elements, as a miraculous source, originating in the human hearts and brains of those who gathered there. The energies of the incarnates mixed each other to the vigorous fluids of workers in our action plan, gathered in vast number, creating precious storages of benefits for the unfortunate, still extremely attached to the physiological sensations (XAVIER, 1982, p. 12).

In the physical effects ones, in particular, it is the fundamental energy to these events, enabling the materialization or dematerialization of beings and things.

A Theory About Ectoplasm's Origin

The ectoplasm originates in the vital principle, captured and modified by the interactive action between the biomagnetic fields of perispirit cells and the magnetic field of physical cells. Since the vital principle has its origin in the vital fluid, it is constantly renewed by absorption, both alimentary and respiratory, as well as through the energy centers of the biome, whose structure would be ectoplasmic.

The source of the vital fluid would be the pantachic frontier between the spiritual universe, or astral, and the material universe. This zone would be characterized by energy instability, where the laws relevant to each one of the dimensions would not work, which would give it a *sui generis* structuring that would provide it with the faculty of performing actions uncommon to these dimensions.

The fundamental substance of the intermediate dimension, which some call etheric, would have the faculty, when associated with the interactive energies of the perispirit and the body, to return the enveloping movement to the atoms of the material universe, lost due to a dimension decreasement caused by the Big Bang. Such a movement, which could be called spin x, returns The Lost Dimension to it, removing it from the physical plane, temporarily or permanently, and placing it on the spiritual plane. This would explain the phenomenon of transport, or dematerialization, as the recovery of spin x, by the physical atoms, under the action of ectoplasm. Similarly, the phenomena of materialization of beings and things of the spiritual world in the physical could be explained by subtracting the spin x of these objects, causing them to fall into our dimension, also under the influx of the same substance.

Acting as to introduce a supradimensional motion in the basic particles of matter, ectoplasm causes an object to be removed from our dimension permanently or transported at such a great speed that space and time are reduced to practically zero, in addition to allowing the placement, or removal, of objects in hermetically sealed enclosures.

It can also act to eliminate a dimension of an object proper to the spiritual world, making it appear in our dimension, in a permanent character, as well as create living organisms in temporality, in whole or in part, under the influence of organic organizing biological models, or structuring fields of the form, human, as well as plant and animal.

Ectoplasm is a substance sensitive to the influence of the mind, extremely plastic, easily shaping itself according to the idealizations of the agent, physical or spiritual, that manipulates it.

Use of Ectoplasm by Human Science

Ectoplasm will be, in the future, the modifying element of the face of the world, causing a complete review of physical, biological and technological knowledge and, consequently, revolutionizing philosophy, the arts and culture in general. Why such statements? Because ectoplasm will provide the following achievements:

a) Creation of instant journeys, when dematerialization and materialization devices, synchronized with specific coordinates, will allow people to move to any part of the world, without time waste.

b) Interplanetary traveling at a speed range superior to light speed, facilitating the study and colonization of stars of our system, or others.

c) Operations that do not harm the body, by simply dematerializing damaged tissues or foreign bodies from the inside of the body and taking it out as well as the application "in loco" of medicine and therapies in any part of the human body.

d) Diagnosis of diseases or injuries within the organic structure, making the tissues transparent within the location where those happen. This skill will allow the live study of all the organic functions, abolishing the cruel system of vivisection.

e) The creation of works of art with four dimensions and of mental reflexes, the limits of which will be dictated by the aesthetics and creativity of artists, as well as the making of revolutionary musical pieces using the faculty of raps and the like.

(f) Construction of cranes and conveyors, using the Crawford Lever principle.

(g) Manufacture of coordinating mechanisms that obey mental controls.

(h) Construction of devices that make thought visible or that enable the creation of three-dimensional mental pictures.

(i) Use of matter-by-matter interpenetration possibilities in the areas of geology, mining, construction, jewelry and manufacturing in general.

This thesis ends here since the possibilities are limitless. I would like to draw attention, however, to the need for large scale artificial ectoplasm production, so that it can be used at an industrial and technical level, although there is the possibility of extracting it from nature and living organisms, through ectoplasmic pickups and capacitors, such as the one built by Jonathan Koons under the guidance of his mentors, in the heroic times of 1848. Worth noting that this transitional energy is present, with its own characteristics, in all frontier zones between consecutive spiritual levels. This way it is possible to speak of Psychosomatic ectoplasm, mental ectoplasm, etc.

6. THE PERISPIRIT

Introduction to the Spiritual Body Concept

In question 93 of The Spirits' Book, it is stated that the spirit is always involved by a substance, which Allan Kardec called *perispirit*, in an analogy with the perisperm that surrounds the seed. Thus, the first rational and objective description of the *spiritual being* in the history of thought arose. The spirit left the domains of pure metaphysical speculation to become objectively and experimentally analyzed. Through spiritist experiments, it was found that the individual's essence, or intelligent principle, is involved by an energy complex that many had already predicted, then calling it the spiritual body, which Kardec later called *perispirit*. This spiritual body has already appeared quoted in Rigveda: *unfold, oh! God, your splendors and thus give the dead the new body in which the soul shall be carried according to Thy Will*; the Egyptians called Ka the involucre of the spirit; in China, it was said that no matter how subtle and imperceptive they are, they (the spirits) manifest themselves through the corporeal shapes of the beings, of a real and true essence which cannot cease to manifest itself under any shapes; among the Jews, the Kabbalah calls the spiritual body Nephesh; Greek philosophers nicknamed it Ochema, while Hippocrates called it Enormon; among the Christians, St. Paul thus expresses himself: *They are buried as natural human bodies, but they will be raised as spiritual bodies. For just as there are natural bodies, there are also spiritual bodies* (I Cor 15, 43-44), and Origenes says that the spiritual body participates in the incarnations of the soul in the various worlds, it being necessary to animate several bodies; Paracelsus, famous alchemist and physician, gave it the name of *astral body* because he found that his tessitura was formed of emanations of the stars.

The Perispirit's Role

The perispirit is the modeling, organizing and managing structure of the physical body; energetic mold where the mechanisms responsible for all organic functions are found, from the selection of hereditary principles to the organization of the egg cell and its development in a complex organism. It contains the phylogenetic matrix that promotes organogenic repetition of the main evolutionary stages of being.

Functional centers live within the perispirit, they direct and control the archetypal emissions of the deep unconscious, therefore generating the physiopsychic functions of the living beings, more specifically of the human species, where they are extraordinarily complex and refined.

The spiritist thinkers, led by Gabriel Delanne (1857-1926) and Léon Denis (1846-1927), (from whom I have extracted these concepts), as well as the most renowned spirits of the Brazilian Spiritist movement, such as Emmanuel and André Luiz (see XAVIER, 1985) defined the biological evolution as the result of an interaction between the perispirit and matter, through the millennia, attaching in it the conditioned reflexes responsible for the structure and management of the organic complex.

The perispirit is the conduit where the results of humankind's evolutionary process are recorded, that is, the result of interactions between beings and the environment. The existential experiences, repeated *ad nauseam*, are attached to it as psychosomatic conditioned reflexes, becoming conductive substrates of the mental and physiological processes.

The mutations, studied by the Dutch botanist Hugo de Vries (1848-1935), whose importance in the mechanism of evolution is immense, implant themselves in the spiritual body when deriving from external factors, or they arise from it, as they are produced by benign or malignant changes induced by the self, through compromising actions of their organizational balance. Worth considering, however, that acts of organic or psychological impact can be expressed through palingenesis as phenotypic manifestations or traits, not based on a natural genetic inheritance, simply because they come to exist because of a temporary organizational disturbance of the spiritual body. The reason why this happens is that the perispirit is the one to coordinate the genetic selection in the formation of the egg cell, as a pre-existing biogenetic fulcrum, it not only selects the chromosomal material of the male and female gametes but also modifies the genetic code itself, reprogramming it according to its structural reality at the moment. Many of these changes occur within a pathological pattern, creating the congenital physiological abnormalities syndromes, as well as those that occur during the existential course, within an extensive list of diverse pathogenies.

Through the contemporary mediumistic studies, as well as through the reflections of remarkable researchers and spiritists thinkers of yore and today, one can understand that the perispirit's activities even include the psychological dimension, not only responsible for controlling the physiological automatism, but also hosting for registering the psychic facts, such as memory, the past and the current unconscious, in short, all mental phenomena. The perispirit organizes itself into many energy levels, which are responsible for physical and psychological manifestation of individuals. However, as the perispirit is an organic complex, the true responsible for the existence and functioning of the being is the intelligent principle, or the spirit itself, a *divine spark, a conscious Ray of God's thoughts.*

The Spirit and its Need of a Body

> Is it correct to say that spirits are immaterial? How can we define something when we have no terms for comparison, and when we only have an insufficient language at our disposal? Can one who is born blind define light? 'Immaterial' is not the right word; 'incorporeal' would be more precise, because you should understand that, since it is a creation, a spirit must be something. A spirit is quintessentialized matter; thus, you have no analogies for describing it. It is also so etherealized that your senses cannot perceive it. (KARDECI, 2007, par. 82).

The consolidating spirits felt the difficulty of defining the intelligent principle and tried to illustrate their ideas using the concept of matter, as understood by Kardec's physics of time. Today, of course, they would use the most advanced concepts of the theory of relativity and quantum theory, assimilating its analogies to the current energy schemes. And of course, we cannot understand what they were trying to convey. Saying that the spirit is something is an extremely vague statement. As for the problem of subtle matter, unable to injure our senses, so it happens to the *spiritual entities* or the spiritual environment, however they are remarkably close to us, in vibratory terms and, as indicated by mediumistic phenomena and revealed by many spirits, they are composed of dissociable particles, which ultimately means that they are material within our current concepts of matter.

I take the liberty to interpret the Consolidated spirits' thought as being the *intelligent principle* very far from us, in terms of *vibrational frequency*, in such a way that it seems immaterial to us, because they are at the extreme opposite to what is material. Due to this existential situation, the intelligent principle has no conditions to act directly on the physical body. Oldest thinkers have already admitted that, assuming the existence of an intermediate substance as necessary to interconnect the two vibrating ends.

With the concept of *Perispirit*, Kardec responds to the question that has always been imposed when one discussed spirit and matter: how could the first, immaterial, act on the second? It places itself as a mediator between one and the other, allowing the traffic between the two opposite conditions of being.

However, the consolidation presents another mediator between the perispirit and the body: the vital fluid or biome. Thus, it is possible to describe the structure of the individual with the following equation:

$$I = e + p + b + s \qquad \text{(VIII)}$$

Where:

I = individual;

e = Spirit, creation's intelligent principle;

p = perispirit;

b = biome or individualized vital fluid;

s = sum (physical body).

Or schematically:

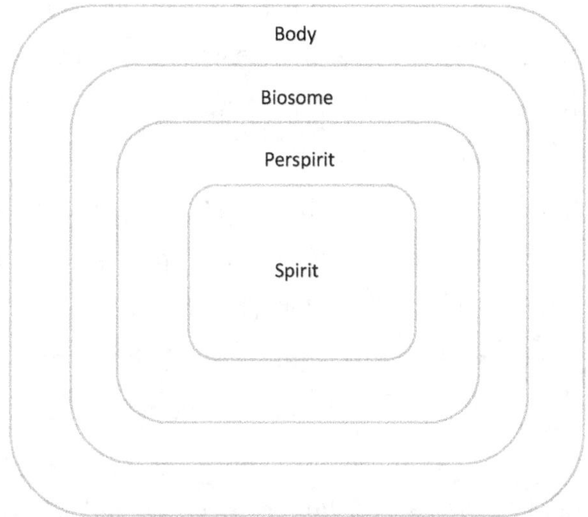

Thus, using the consolidating spirits' definition, the being is formed by a distinct energetic complex that allows a synergetic connection between the human being's essence, the *intelligent principle*, and the body.

Reasoning about the expression (VIII), we can frame b and s as integral parts of the perispirit, since they are equally involucres of the spirit, although the involucre is, in this case, debatable: $p = b + s$. Thus, we may have a variation of (VIII):

$$I = e + p \qquad \text{(IX)}$$

As it turns out, the human being ceases to be a binomial, as traditional religions wanted, to divide itself into a quaternary of energies differentiated by gradation. To link the intelligent principle to the body, a *plastic mediator* is needed; however, it takes an intermediary link for it to work: the vital principle. As seen, it is generated by the action of energies produced in the frontier Zone between spiritual and material dimensions.

The Perispirit's Structure

Perispirit, as seen in the consolidation, places us before a paradox: on one hand, it is as immaterial as the intelligent principle, so it would be able to interact with it; and, on the other hand, it is so dense that it has the property of guiding the generation, maintenance and control of the physical organic complex. It would therefore have to enjoy a functional duality: to be almost material and almost immaterial, simultaneously: which seems to us an absurdity. It even recalls the ether of pre-Einsteinian physics that should have elasticity and not provide the slightest resistance, a paradox that did not resist the experiences of Michelson (1852-1931) and Morley (1839-1923) and was eventually replaced by the relativistic field theory.

The experimental results around the perispirit, carried out between the last decade of the nineteenth century and the beginning of the twentieth century, demonstrated that it has a much more complex structure than initially thought.

The set of perispirit energy levels has been laboratory proven by several researchers, and they have exposed their diverse conformation in the context of gradually condensed energies:

In 1893, Colonel De Rochas D'Aiglun externalized the biome, or double etheric, demonstrating that sensitivity can be displaced from the organism. Hector Durville, in 1909, acting magnetically on the externalized biome, isolated the psychosome, or astral body, of Paracelsus. Dr. Baraduc, well known for the thought's photographic experiences, registered the existence of another energy level of the perispirit, which he called the mental body, successfully externalized by L. Lefranc, a disciple of Durville, in 1912. Durville and Lefranc introduced the magnetization technique on exteriorized bodies, in order to achieve the emergence of a new stratum. In 1912, Lefranc dissociated the causal body. Due to the employment of a method he called synthetic, Lancelin achieved the unfolding of other energy levels which he named: moral Soul, intuitive soul and, finally, conscientious soul, but he was not able to continue the exteriorizations beyond this point (see Freire, 1956).

These experiments demonstrated that the perispirit is formed by differentiated energy levels of the body's *intelligent principle*, which are then distributed according to their increasing density. This places the perispirit back into a logical conceptualization and solves the problem of its nature. Theosophists, starting from the discoveries of the Hindu rishis, had already described these levels as *spiritual bodies*.

In our days, the spirit André Luiz, through the medium Francisco Cândido XAVIER, refers to the *individualized vital fluid*, the *biome*, to the *psychosome* and the *mental body,* the mental some. He also tells us that the *psychosome*, like the *soma* and the *biome*, can suffer pathological changes and even *die*. According to the exposed, the Incarnate individual would possess, roughly speaking, the following Constitution:

Inteligent Principle		
Supramental energetics levels		
Mental Level	Superconscious	
	Conscious	
	Subconscious	
Psychosoma		
Biosome or Etheric Double		
Body		

Dr. Jorge Andréa dos Santos proposes another classification (Santos, 1987, pp. 22):

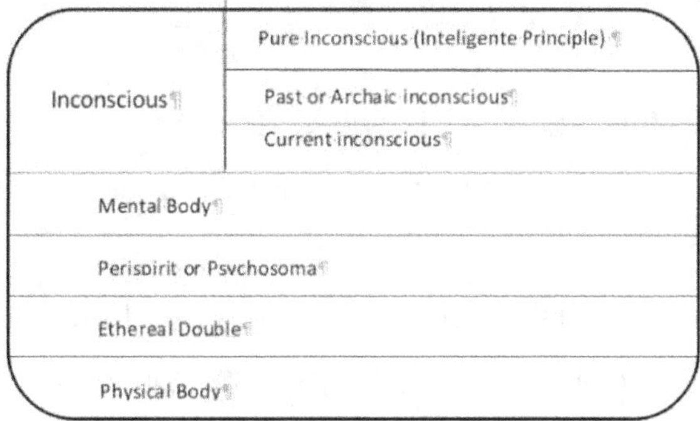

Inconscious	Pure Inconscious (Inteligente Principle)
	Past or Archaic Inconscious
	Current inconscious
Mental Body	
Perispirit or Psychosoma	
Ethereal Double	
Physical Body	

I want to present another scheme. It is based on the psychic sphere of analytical psychology. This scheme is complementary to those that have been exposed above, because psychism, in my opinion, is the result of the interaction between all the processes that occur within the level that form the individual, as well as between themselves.

Intelligent Principle	Selfs'Archetype	collective Unconsious
	Archetypes Instincts	
Level N	Record of past	Arcaic Unconscious
Level N-1	Existences	
Level …		
Level …	Current Unconscious	
Level …	Complexes	
Level N-n		
Biossome	Ego	
Physichal Body	Conscious	

In the scheme, the relations between the perispirit's levels and its psychic correspondents are not accurate, so they should be better defined. But I think I have exposed my point of view.

The result of what has just been seen is that, alike the spiritual universes, the many energetic levels of the perispirit show a progressive condensation, which demonstrates that they are linked between themselves.

A proper psychosomatic level corresponds to each dimensional level, through which the spirit can experience its realities in its evolutionary process.

Thus, one can say that:

$$P = \sum_{i=1}^{N} N_i \qquad \text{(X)}$$

Where

p = Perispirit

N = perispiritual stratum, in density gradation.

One can rewrite (IX):

$$I = E . \sum_{i=1}^{N} N_i \qquad \text{(XI)}$$

Or considering the physical body separately:

$$I = E \left(\sum_{i=1}^{N} N_i \right) + S \qquad \text{(XII)}$$

Where S = Somatic Body.

As the densities of the perispirit layers are increasing, we can imagine them in constant gradation, which would allow us to view them in a series similar to a finite arithmetic progression, unfolding from N_1 to N_{n-1}, with a ratio r, where: $r = N_n - N_{n-1}$

Applying the formula for the sum of arithmetic progression (VII), one reaches:

$$P = (N_1 + N_n) \, r/2 \qquad \text{(XIII)}$$

which would represent the set of energy levels that form the perispirit, when analyzed in a bi-dimensional view. In addition, I seek to study the process as a discrete distribution, to facilitate the approach, however, the perispiritual set will represent a continuous distribution, where we will find, similar to the universal scheme, frontier zones, with the intersection between two consecutive levels, generating a transition band, known as individualized vital fluid of each level, i.e.:

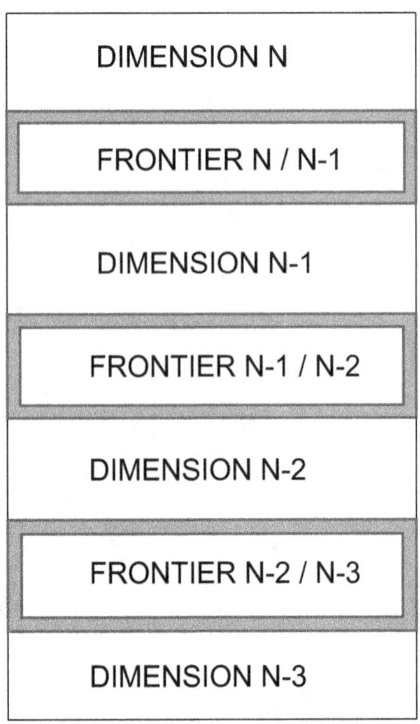

According to the above, it is possible to understand why mediumship happens, also, in the spiritual dimensions. Those who live in a dimension are in fact incarnated in it, that is, they use a body of their own for that dimension. At the same time, they exist in another higher dimension, which means that the body used at the moment is also disposable as the physical body is for us. In the same way as among humans, the dissociation between the upper and lower somatic body (psychosome and physical body) provides mediums the contact with those who live in the higher dimension and serves as an intermediary for their messages. At least, according to André Luiz, who talked about his experience. He said that, secluded in a comfortable and spacious room, he prayed to the Lord of Life thanking him for the blessing of having been helpful, mentioning that the "fruitful fatigue" of those who do their duty gave him no opportunity for any unpleasant vigil. From that, sensations of lightness had invaded his whole soul and he had the impression of being caught in a small boat, heading to Unknown Regions. He asked where he was headed but felt as if it were impossible to answer. Next to him, a silent man held the helm... After a few minutes, he found himself in front of a wonderful port, where someone called him with special affection: Andre!... André!... He then disembarked with truly childish precipitation... And then he saw himself hugging his mother in overflows of joy (XAVIER, 1988, p. 196).

It is a singular dream because it happens in the spiritual world. The author tells how, after his first day of work in the spiritual city where he was living, he laid down, immediately slept, and dreamt about the same aspects of symbolism (the boat sailing and The Boatman at the helm), something that was to be expected, since the deep subconscious is active. The description of the dream, made by André Luiz, is a precious indication because it did not exactly match what happens on Earth. He knew perfectly well that he had left the lower body in the apartment of the rectification Chambers, in 'Our Home', and had absolute awareness of that movement. His notions of space and time were exact. The richness of emotions, in turn, became more and more intense (XAVIER, 2003, pp.198).

He was therefore unfolded. He was perfectly aware that the lower body remained where it laid. A dream phenomenon, like spiritual unfolding, similar to what the incarnates experience (for an analysis of this dream see ARGOLLO, 2005, pp. 208-213). If dissociable, the mentioned body is disposable, like the physical body, and it is what the same author calls Psychosoma, in *Evolving in Two Worlds* and *Mechanisms of Mediumship*, when mentioning that other times, rare indeed, he had heard news from friends who had lost the perispiritual body, achieving higher planes. In addition: the perispirit, later, will be the object of more expansive studies in Christian schools. I only disagree with the spiritual author when he names perispirit a spiritual body that is able to die, but, as I have already mentioned, he rectified this in subsequent books. Thus, justified when, based on him, and on other incarnated authors and researchers, as already seen, I visualize the perispirit as a set of differentiated energy levels, in varying density. However, since an upper body has to act on the lower, naturally it is possible to imagine a specific vital principle for each of these levels, and its result can be externalized, as an ectoplasm, providing the materialization of higher entities, which are embodied, thus in the less elevated dimension. André Luiz himself cites numerous similar facts, and I invite my readers to check it, reviewing the works of this remarkable, and still unknown spiritual scientist who, paradoxically, is the most read.

To illustrate what I have just said about spiritual bodies, let us review what the already mentioned spiritual author once stated. He said that in order to define the spiritual body in some way, it is necessary to consider, first of all, that it is not the reflection of the physical body, because, in reality, it is the physical body that reflects it, as much as itself, the spiritual body portrays in itself the mental body that presides over its formation (XAVIER, 1985, p. 25).

In order to clarify, he says that the mental body, experimentally pointed out by several scholars, is the subtle involucre of the mind, and that, for the time being, they could not define with more breadth of conceptualization beyond the one with which it had been presented by the Incarnate researchers, due to a lack of adequate terminology in the terrestrial dictionary (XAVIER, 1985, p. 25, footnote no. 8).

7. MEDIUMSHIP AND EVOLUTION

Preliminary Questions

Medium is a gender-neutral Latin word (there is no female for *medium*) that means: *mean, intermediate, conduit,* etc. Due to its own etymology, it does not have, nor is it allowed to have, any other usage rather than that inherent meaning. *Mediumship* is the medium's proper faculty. Medium is everyone whose spiritual faculty is used by disembodied spirits, in order to intervene in the physical world. Currently, the concepts of medium and mediumship are applied to any and all psychic phenomena, even those that are produced by the mediums themselves, without aid from spiritual agents. This happens because there are no unanimously accepted terms to indicate both. As long as there is no effective and definitive way to prove whether a psychic fact is produced by the one who possesses the faculty or if by a disembodied spirit, what is the problem of using the term for both? Simply not using, or systematically criticizing this usage, for the sake of prejudice, because of its link to the continuity of existence, or to pose as a scientist, is childish, which only demonstrates immaturity or extreme need for appreciation.

Universality of the Mediumistic Faculty

Allan Kardec's advantage over almost all of those who had studied spiritist phenomena before and after him was following the natural process of its development. The consolidator did not seek to frame the phenomena in preconceived ideas, he simply got carried away, since the phenomenon is intelligent, only analyzing, criticizing and choosing according to convergence proof criteria, where the statistical method applies to the feature. He accepted the new knowledge within its own defining parameters, not worrying too much with what the scientific community of his time might want or think. The important thing is the truth, not the particular damage of cultured castes. Allan Kardec defines medium as:

> Every individual who senses the influence of spirits to any degree of intensity is a medium. This faculty is inherent to humankind. It, therefore, does not constitute an exclusive privilege, and there are very few individuals who do not possess it at least in a rudimentary state. Thus, we can state that everyone is a medium to a certain degree. Usually, however, this label is applied solely to those who possess a well-characterized mediumistic faculty that expresses itself through patent

For Kardec, in this excerpt, mediumship is practically universal: therefore, one can say that *nearly everyone is a medium*, the name being applied to those who *present evident effects*, for the sake of common use, very natural. The Master of Lyon could not sharply distinguish the medium and the psychic – this includes individuals who possess paranormal faculties and that exercise them by their own free will – simply because this distinction does not exist. *Every psychic is a medium, and every medium is a sensitive,* this is an important psychic law because, like all natural principles, one can reverse it. *Sensitive*, as well as a *psychic*, are so-called *scientific* denominations, created to name individuals who have sensibility to perceive transcendent phenomena.

Kardec wrote about the *sensitive* or *impressionable mediums*, which are the mediums that feel the presence of spirits through vague impressions, a kind of shiver on the whole body. Well, the sensitivity is, for mediumship, as tact is for the other senses, it is the basic Matrix. The individual already presents a mediumistic characteristic simply due to the fact of feeling something transcendent. There is not, in the whole history of Psychic Studies, *a sensitive whom has not experienced mediumistic facts, in the same way, that it would be impossible to find a medium that would not be, first of all, a sensitive, because the two faculties enjoy the commutative properties.*

Ernesto Bozzano clarifies that mediumship is a faculty proper to all human beings because it is the exteriorization of subconscious faculties, and which natural disposition, diseases, accidents, or the proximity of death can update. He once said that the supranormal subconscious faculties constitute the spiritual senses of the subconscious personality, senses that will have to appear and exercise in an appropriate environment after death (BOZZANO, 1951, pp. 34). In other words, they are senses proper to the perispirit, to be used in an appropriate environment, that is, in the spiritual world. Consequently, as we are all incarnate spirits, we are all *latently Paranormal* and, as Kardec said, *more or less medium*. The Consolidator, however, after the restriction mentioned above, expands the universe of mediumistic faculty, when referring to the mediumship of inspiration: *In this sense, we could say that all are mediums since there are none who do not have their protector and familiar spirits, who do everything they can to transmit good thoughts to their wards* (KARDEC, 2007, par. 182).

And, finally, he gives us a precious indication: Moreover, for the medium, this faculty is the most susceptible of being developed with practice (KARDEC, 2012, Ch. XV par. 178). This statement has two meanings: one refers to the constant use of the mediumistic faculty, which gradually becomes safer and, of course, more reliable; the other is, since it is a faculty present in all beings when exercised with perseverance and responsibility, tends to manifest itself more strongly with time.

The production of the phenomenon (all spiritists have always agreed) can have its genesis in a spirit — and keep in mind that Kardec, in the excerpt quoted earlier, does not specify whether incarnate or disembodied spirit —, in another, or in the medium itself. It was this second case called *animism* by Von Hartmann, German philosopher that, by excess, attributed all mediumistic phenomena to the medium. It is clear that theoretically there are phenomena produced by the own individual, with no need to speak of conscious or unconscious mystification. It is up to those who make it a war horse to establish the means to define, beyond any reasonable doubt, when a spiritist phenomenon is related to the soul or not. Usually what you read or hear about it is nothing more word-juggling, or rhetorical artifices.

The Problem of *Electrical* People

When addressing *mediums of physical effects*, Kardec also analyzes *involuntary* or *natural mediums*, according to his own classification, saying that they are those whose phenomena occur to, silently. As the case of the poltergeists, today so studied, when the epicenter, or medium, at whose expense the phenomenon occurs, does not have any idea that they are providing the spirits with conditions so that they can act on matter, such as they do. The recommendation of the Consolidator is that the involuntary mediums must be transformed into *facultative mediums*, i.e., in mediums who are aware of their psychic power and who produce the phenomena: *the facultative mediums are those who are aware of their power and who produce the spiritist phenomena by act of their will* (KARDEC, 2012, par. 160).

After considerations on the superiority of facultative mediums over those that willingly produce phenomena, regarding a better exploitation of the faculty, Kardec addresses the problem of electrical people:

> It would seem that to this mediumistic category belong those persons gifted with a certain charge of natural electricity, who are veritable human torpedoes, producing the effects of attraction and repulsion through simple contact. However, it would be erroneous

to regard them as mediums, since true mediumship supposes the direct intervention of a spirit, and experiments have conclusively shown that in this particular case electricity is the only agent behind the phenomena. This strange faculty, which may almost always be regarded as an illness, can sometimes be linked to mediumship, as seen in the case of the Spirit-rapper of Bergzabern; however, most of the time it is completely independent. According to what we have stated, the sole proof of spirit intervention is the intelligent character of the manifestations. Whenever this factor is absent, it is most logical to attribute the phenomena to purely physical causes. The question still remains as to whether electrical persons might have a greater aptitude for becoming physical effects mediums. We believe they would, but only experience will verify it (KARDEC, 2012, par. 163).

Electrical people, as Kardec analyzes, would be endowed with the ability to store electricity and, because of that, attract or repel objects. Therefore, the Faculty of which they are carriers lies in a physical problem because electricity is not a psychic subject. When walking, for example, clothes, and even the body itself, get charged with static electricity, being able to produce attractions and repulsions, according to the laws of electricity and magnetism. Would Kardec, while analyzing these people, be keeping in mind what happened to *Angelique Cottin*? This fourteen-year-old girl presented, since January 15, 1846, the Faculty of having furniture and objects move while in her presence, reaching a point when she could no longer weave silk cloths, which was her work. Since the beginning of the investigations, it was assumed that electricity was the cause of the phenomenon. However, when the Paris Academy of Sciences appointed a committee, composed of Arago, who had already been a witness to the phenomena, Henri Becquerel, Geoffroy Saint-Hilaire, Babinet, Rayer and Pariset, all renowned wiseman, equipped with the best appliances of the time, to see if the facts had electrical genesis, the phenomena did not happen, because the girl was frightened. Now, if it were a simple physical phenomenon, this would not have happened.

The electrical hypothesis, in the case of Angelique, was the fruit of haste from those who first witnessed the events, in fact, she was a natural or involuntary medium of physical effects and did not look like a human replica of electric eels. In her presence, a *simple Poltergeist phenomenon* took place, as can be seen with a careful study of the information that has been provided. It is interesting to note that the phenomena had periods of great intensity and periods where nothing happens, and eventually ended up ceasing completely. When the girl had become frightened, as before the wiseman of the Academy, they completely ceased. Studies with mediums, in whose presence infestations take place, demonstrate that, generally, they are young people in full bloom of sexual energies, such as in the case of Angelique, and who have psychic problems such as neuroses, feelings of rejection, emotional delusions, etc. The question arises: do they act like this on their own? It has already been seen that no because they do not know that they produce the movements around them. Would there be spirits acting for them to happen? If they do not present intelligent character, whether this is volition or objective, there is no telling. However, the opposite cannot be said, since, just as they attract public curiosity, they also attract the curiosity of spirits that wander through erraticity. If they did not act at the beginning of them, then they will probably act in the continuation, since, according to *The Spirits' Book*, it is the spirits that *usually direct us*, given the influence and interference they have in our life.

A complete deception is committed by those who seek to define electrical people as an example of exclusively psychic former individuals, that is, able to produce transcendent phenomena on their own, without the aid of the spirits. Now, first of all, we have to prove that these people are psychics, or if they just possess a physical-chemical structure that makes them electricity accumulators. It is a common fact that people get charged with static electricity, simply due to friction with the wind. How often does one get a shock when shaking someone's hand? Finally, *who can guarantee those electrical people, if psychics, produce phenomena exclusively for themselves? Who desires to know, with absolute certainty, which spiritual entities do not produce them?* Therefore, this argument only shows that the fact has not been properly studied.

Would Mediumship be an Evolutionary Process?

The most varied hypotheses have been issued to explain the mediumistic faculty. The first, and most simplistic one, is the one that denies its existence. It can even be said that it is earlier than the Hydesville phenomena since it is the trench of those who, in general, do not have the least knowledge of transcendent phenomena. It is the easy choice of the prejudiced, lazy, doubtful, or simply ignorant.

Among those who decide to research the subject, it is necessary to select those who do it superficially, therefore their conclusions suffer from natural deviations because they lack breadth and depth; others, suffering from ideological shortsightedness, accept the facts, but attribute them to the devil and its army, when these happen outside the dogmatic sphere of their beliefs, for those who ascribe them there, are due to the intervention of God, disguised as a mysterious *Holy Spirit*. After all, the Truth only exists in and for them, the elect ones, exclusive heirs of the Kingdom of Heaven; as can be seen, a mere case of blind fanaticism, amenable to fitting in some psychopathological category. At this same level, historical materialists must be placed, for they think only according to the undisputed dogmas of their patrons: Marx and Engels, whose words and concepts they mechanically repeat, in a monotonous monoideism, stuck to self-sustaining and idealist tautologies. Leaving aside these social strata, whose value of opinion is none, because easily refutable, I turn to those who, sincerely and honestly, have studied mediumistic phenomenology. They can be divided into materialists (where we include even those who, calling themselves spiritualists, opt for physical-psychological explanations) and spiritists (all those who are disembodied spirits who communicate through mediums, although they do not follow the principles consolidated by Allan Kardec). The first ones attribute mediumistic communications to the medium, whose unconscious mind turns into a fantastic entity, capable of accessing the hidden places of someone's unconscious, however distant as it may be, they call this faculty telemnesia. In general, psychic phenomena themselves are used to try to explain the mediumistic facts. Clairvoyance and telepathy form the theoretical support of this theory, which receives the generic name of animism, proposed by the German philosopher Von Hartmann in 1885, a disciple of Schopenhauer, who referred to the phenomena of the *animal magnetism*, as quoted by the young Jung, in the student fraternity Zofingia, in Basel, Switzerland:

> As my second ally, I cite Arthur Schopenhauer, who states in his Parerga und Paralipomena: "It is not my vocation to combat the skepticism of ignorance whose caviling deportment brings it into disrepute every day". "Nowadays anyone who doubts the fact of animal magnetism and the clairvoyance it confers, must not be called skeptical but ignorant". Schopenhauer wrote this almost fifty years ago (JUNG, 1983, p. 25).

Despite the refutation of Alexander Aksakof in 1890, which was definitive, the opponents of the spirit's existence continue to repeat it, as if nothing had happened (see AKSAKOF, 1956).

Among those who accept the exogenous spiritual presence as a determinant of psychic facts, some hypotheses try to explain it: a) mediumship as a residue of atavistic faculties, atrophied because of natural selection, which would have rendered it useless; b) aborted rudiments of senses that have never developed, nor will develop, since they're useless to the species, to the struggle for survival; c) sense germs developing until permanently attached to a body; d) a particular faculty, of some individuals, not necessarily common to all (BOZZANO, 1951, pp. 16-17).

Bozzano's answer is overwhelmingly logical. It starts by demonstrating that mediumship cannot be linked to biological evolution, which presupposes hypotheses a, b and c. First, if mediumship were part of the senses, in the early human stages, it would have been very useful, because, as is known, men have always sought to know what is going on in the minds of opponents, to better attack them or defend themselves from attacks. Worthy of note is that this craving is present, as it always has been, in the normal life of relationships. In the everyday life of existence, traders always try to guess what goes on in the mind of opponents; jealous lovers, what happens in the mind of their beloved, and vice versa; the student, the answer to the question that they ask the teacher; the general, what the enemy thinks, and so on. On this side, it is realized how much mediumship, if linked to organic evolution, would have support to establish itself as a definitive achievement of the species. Why, however, has it not been, nor can it be? Bozzano's answer analyses the situation in which the phenomena occur: the biological abnormality one, that is, at the moment of mediumistic perception, the individual is in a state of partial or total suspension of vital functions or, as it is said nowadays, in an altered state of consciousness. This state, by itself, would be an impediment so that natural selection would establish it as a biological conquest of the human being, at the mercy of its natural enemies. A function that inhibits protective Biological reflexes is a pernicious factor to the species, perhaps, for this reason, Bozzano is correct in eliminating mediumship as a primeval faculty or evolving in humans.

On the other hand, the emergence of mediumistic perceptions in cases of accidents, diseases, or proximity to death, in individuals who have never demonstrated it in a normal situation of their lives, is the proof that it exists in the unconscious of all, in a latent state. Hence, the Italian spiritist philosopher states: mediumistic perceptions are not part of our biological context, nor past nor future, but it is about the manifestation of senses that concern the spiritual being in us, and proper to the spiritual habitat, where they have full application. This gracious idea meets the exact substrate of the thesis dealt with in this book. The spiritual being, in order to see in its four-dimensional context, needs an own sensory organization, adapted to the environment where it lives and develops itself.

Allan Kardec treats the psychosomatic organizations according to the consolidation spirits, in *The Spirits' Book*, mainly in the *Theoretical Essay on Sensations in Spirits*, where it is clear that all spiritual perceptions have a global character, that is, they happen throughout the organ-psychic organization, with no rigorous specializations, as in the physical organism. What is more, living in a four-dimensional environment (the spiritual world immediate to the Earth's crust), all sensations should happen in three-dimensional configurations, being treated by the spiritual mind as a four-dimensional set.

Here is an analogy between perceptions in the spiritual world, and physical sensations, which are produced in a two-dimensional situation, but are elaborated in the brain from a three-dimensional perspective: vision. In our dimension, the eyeball receives the projection of a two-dimensional image, but the brain, analyzing light and shadow, gives it a three-dimensional treatment. In the four-dimensional world of spirits, vision should be received by the spiritual body as a three-dimensional image, but the spiritual brain will treat it in a four-dimensional perspective, that is, the vision will encompass the whole object, as if seen from all angles, simultaneously giving it also highlight proximity. In another excellent monograph, Bozzano, when transcribing a narration of a spirit about its own death and first moments in the spiritual world, tells us that the landscape was flat and undulating, very similar, in certain points of view, to the rural beauties of its dear parents in the world of the living. However, the most wonderful detail of the panorama contemplated were the distant objects that did not seem in any way diminished in their proportions, due to the effect of distances, as happens in the terrestrial environment. The perspective presented itself literally transformed. Moreover, it was not all, because the spirit then verified that it simultaneously perceived objects on all sides and not only on the side exposed to its view, as it happens in the world of the living. This amplified and improved faculty of vision produces wonderful effects. When observing the outer surface from any object, one sees its interior, its outline and, through it, what is beyond it, from which it follows that the spiritual vision puts the Observer in conditions of fully penetrate the observed object. (BOZZANO, 1962, pp. 79-80).

Later, in another narration of the spiritual world, it is mentioned that in the world of the living, the sense of sight puts the Observer in a state of viewing only one side, one aspect of the observed object. There, spirits see the object simultaneously from all sides. It means that when they look at something, they do not just see it as we see it: they penetrate it in all its parts. They see around and through it, what makes they come, in an instant, to have complete knowledge of what might interest them (BOZZANO, 1962, pp.84).

It is shown that visual perception expands, in the world of spirits, as a result of the ability to perceive and mentally elaborate the fourth vector of this dimension. The descriptions draw attention to the change in the perspective we have gotten used to, which shows only one face of the visualized object. One also acquires the ability to see in and through things, as well as how to perceive them in their real dimensions, despite the distance. This last revelation puts us before the problem of the exact meaning of space in the Spiritual World, which can explain a series of phenomena provoked by spirits, in our world through mediumship, where space and time seem to be absent or to be literally nullified.

8. STUDIES ON THE SPIRIT

The Spirit: Biological and Psychological Concepts

In the field of Biology, a materialistic conception regarding the spirit has prevailed as a rule. Therefore, it would only be a result of physical-chemical interactions in the body, a mere epiphenomenon of the physiological metabolism.

Neo-Darwinism seeks to employ the philosophical consequences of quantum concepts to the emergence of morphological and structural characters of living beings, seeing them as a probabilistic product of chance. However, the need for attaching the characters, as a result of the biosphere context, arises from the interaction between the external pressures of the environment and the internal pressure of the species: *For the selective pressures exerted by outside conditions upon organisms are in no case unconnected with the teleonomic performances characteristic of the species* (MONOD, 1972, pp. 125), as Jacques Monod assures. Therefore, evolution is conceptualized, as a stochastic and deterministic process, simultaneously. There is, according to this perspective, no metaphysical agent (God or spirit) acting in the processes, neither creatively nor as a maintainer.

In order to deepen the reductionism knowledge that had started to take over the area of organic Studies, Richard Dawkins says:

> Like successful Chicago gangsters, our genes have survived, in some cases for millions of years, in a highly competitive world. These entities us to expect certain qualities in our genes. I shall argue that a predominant quality to be expected in a successful gene is ruthless selfishness. This gene selfishness will usually give rise to selfishness in individual behavior. However, as we shall see, there are special circumstances in which a gene can achieve its own selfish goals best by fostering a limited form of altruism at the level of individual animals. But Dawkings, aware of the type of ethics that evolves from his theory, searches a way out, starting with an analogy with the molecule that replicates the DNA: the meme, that is, a replicator that is still under developing in a primordial culture broth, and developing at great speed, surpassing the gene of much. The meme would be a unit of cultural transmission or a unit of imitation: "Just as genes propagate themselves in the gene pool by leaping from body to body via sperms or eggs, so memes propagate themselves in the meme pool by leaping from brain to brain via a process which, in the broad sense, can be called imitation" (DAWKINS, 1989, pp. 192).

These hypotheses, born from analogies with relativistic and quantum concepts, aim to keep the spirit out of discussion as a fundamental entity in the existential drama and, simultaneously, exile the idea of a first, transcendent and immanent cause, creator and maintainer of all things. Regarding the theory of chance, a lottery, I recall the answer of the consolidating spirits to Kardec: *whom that is possessed of common sense can regard chance as an intelligent agent? And, besides, what is chance? Nothing* (KARDEC, 2007, Question 8).

Nowadays, however, the scientists, from the field of Physics, have been trying to reintroduce chance as a factor of creation and transformation. Intra-atomic phenomena would obey to an immense cosmic game of chance. They talk at length about particles that arise from nowhere, resuming the medieval affirmations of creation *ex nihilo*, long-forgotten according to Epicurus and Lucretius: *ex nihilo nihil* (from nothing, nothing or nothing comes from nothing).

Some ingenious theories try to explain such an event, like that of Paul Dirac, about the space formed by virtual particles, which, at times, can acquire enough energy to become real, even for brief seconds. It would be much easier to explain an event of this kind taking into account, as in fact there is, a universe of greater dimension than ours, with which we have generalized borders, through where the traffic of particles can happen, in both directions. Some lose the four-dimensional vector, falling into our three-dimensional universe. Its appearance seems to originate from nothing because, in a region free of particles, one or a swarm of them would appear all of a sudden. The same should happen in the spiritual universe, with three-dimensional particles that, under the influence of the frontier zone, are captured and gain a four-dimensional enveloping that will lead to the finding that, suddenly, in our universe, one or more particles that exist in a given space simply disappear, like a ghost, with no further explanation.

Losing its mysterious character, the creation from nothing ceases to apply to biologists, since the living beings are composed of psychic entities, pre-existing, which undergo transformations, implying changes in the physical body that they structure, through the constant returns to physical existence. In the same way, the genetic mutations, induced by environmental factors, are attached to the psychic organism, nevertheless, however embryonic it is, allowing the emergence of a new acquisition of the species, because the psychic being, returning to a new existence, will build a differentiated organism, alongside the altered matrix that it keeps in itself. Evolution, mutation and adaptation of species, as well as the law of natural selection, are processes that reach not only the physical form, transient, but also the spiritual, that is permanent, and therefore the process can function with the precision and the logic we know.

Necessity can be translated as the teleological impulse that pushes all beings, directing them towards constant improvement. It is not a blind and deterministic physical law, but a much broader law: the law of progress, the director of the universes and the beings that live in them.

The theory of the selfish gene places us in the domains of fantasy. This reductionist way of thinking about nature, turning the entire biosphere into a mere servant of unmistakable, egocentric and amoral DNA molecules, is a schizophrenic delirium. But according to Dawkins, my way of seeing the problem must be a maneuver of my genes, to keep them hidden. It is a cover-up to keep them undiscovered. As if it would do any good, for, as Dawkins says, we are machines that produce and sustain genes, therefore, they have no reason to fear us. Under its tyrannical control, we have no chance of escaping, even with the cultural duplicator molecule, invented as a possible escape from this dictatorship of the intracellular working-class.

It will not take long, and the theory of the egocentric quark will appear, advocating that the whole universe is a machine that produces, maintains and propagates quarks. Everything that happens has its origin in the quark, even The Iliad and The Odyssey, The Bible, the achievements of Science, of Humanism, etc. As it turns out, the imbalance can be contagious...

Let us understand, in a few lines, how Psychology, which paradoxically is — due to vocabulary origin — the science that studies the soul, achieves the prodigy of finding a materialistic foundation for explaining the soul (psyche). In a direct evolution of the French psychiatric thought, influenced by Charcot, emerged, in 1893, the psychoanalysis, with Sigmund Freud. Since Breuer's observations, with patient Anna O., It had been proven that physical problems could have a psychic origin. Freud, when applying a hypnosis mix with mesmerism, mentioned: *I then removed her pains by stroking her a few times across the epigastrium* (FREUD, Complete Works, vol. II, pp. 62). In the first edition there was no "stroking", but rather "applying the healing touch", naturally modified due to 'scientific' questions, since "healing touch" could compromise the 'master'.

Freud was one of the great pioneers of the psyche's studies that have established, in an incontrovertible way, the mastery of the psyche upon physical episodes. In fact, he has assured the existence of a real empire of the psychic over the somatic, radicalizing his positions, which have been more and more reassured. The Viennese physician reached, experimentally, the existence of unconscious mental processes, about which many had already written, mainly Frederic Myer (1843-1901), studying psychic phenomena, with his colleagues from the Society for Psychical Research. As far as the spirit is concerned, it is good to make it clear that the Viennese physician was materialistic, that is, for him, the soul was nothing but an epiphenomenon, although it would exercise decisive influence on organic events. Freud initially intended to deny psychic phenomena peremptorily. However, constant references to facts of telepathic communications, and other psychic experiences, with the patients and between patients and therapists, who arrived to him from all points of the Earth, led him to, reluctantly, accept telepathy, totally rejecting precognition, because it seemed to violate all scientific principles. The explanations of Freudian psychoanalysis for medium and psychic phenomena are mere claims of hallucination, schizophrenia, subliminal romance, hyperesthesia, unconscious movements, paramnesia, elaboration of posteriori, multiple personalities, etc. All inconceivable, the result of little or no observation, but of too much prejudice. These are merely essays to explain isolated episodes and which, even so, are wrong due to their shallowness.

However, Freudian psychoanalysis' disciples, such as Jan Ehrenwald, had the courage to study psychic phenomena, which had happened in their clinical experiences. Jan later fearlessly published his works (EHRENWALD, 1961). Jung, who for a few years had worked with Freud, characterizes the soul and spirit as complex: *The parallel with the primitive belief in souls and spirits is obvious: souls correspond to the autonomous complexes of the personal unconscious, and spirits to those of the collective unconscious* (JUNG, 1984, par. 591);

just as the feeling of the Self: *For this reason, I do not speak simply of the ego, but of an ego-complex, on the proven assumption that the ego, having a fluctuating composition, is changeable and therefore cannot be simply the ego* (JUNG, 1984, par. 611). In order to understand, one must try to comprehend what a complex is, what Jung once defined as: *It is the image of a certain psychic situation which is strongly accentuated emotionally and is, moreover, incompatible with the habitual attitude of consciousness.* (JUNG,1984, par. 201). Defining himself, however, as a reductionist in psychology, Jung radicalizes:

> Spirits are complexes of the collective unconscious which appear when the individual loses his adaptation to reality, or which seek to replace the inadequate attitude of a whole people by a new one. They are therefore either pathological fantasies or new but as yet unknown ideas (JUNG, 1984, par. 597).

As seen, it is more of the same scientific arguments, in which incongruity becomes logic and a commonplace turns into the foundation of Reason. However, psychic phenomena began to impose themselves on the academic community, especially after Parapsychology, and Jung, as an honest thinker and scientist, could not stay aloof from the subject, shielding himself with pathological hypotheses, since the experiments of Rhine and his collaborators took place according to probabilistic norms. In addition, probability started to be recognized, due to the quantum theory, amongst the traditional scientific means.

Due to the discoveries of Physics in the macro and microcosmic fields, the traditional epistemological concepts had undergone considerable change. Based on this, in his personal experience and study of paranormal facts, Jung developed, alongside Wolfgang Pauli (1900-1958) – Nobel Prize in Physics – the concept of *Synchronicity*, which he called a *hypothetical explanation equivalent to causality*, because of its character of simultaneity. Parapsychological phenomena, studied and scientifically proven by Rhine, had a considerable weight in structuring this concept:

> Rhine's experiments confront us with the fact that there are events which are related to one another experimentally, and in this case meaningfully, with-out there being any possibility of proving that this relation is a causal one, since the "transmission" exhibits none of the known properties of energy (JUNG, 2005, par. 840).

As Rhine did, Jung sought to clearly and simply delimitate the field of his study. He stated that synchronic events rest on the simultaneity of two different psychic states. One of them is the normal, probable state (i.e., the one that is causally explicable), and the other, that is, critical experience, cannot causally derive from the first (Jung, 2005, par. 855). And Jung clarifies this by saying: *An unexpected content which is directly or indirectly connected with some objective external event coincides with the ordinary psychic state: this is what I call synchronicity* (JUNG, 2005, par. 855).

Therefore, one must be careful when labeling some unusual events, especially paranormal ones, of synchronicity. For example, a common mediumistic phenomenon cannot be called synchronicity, unless its objective occurrence was accompanied by a correlated psychic state. I have been tempted to add *and simultaneous*, but Jung emphasizes the *relativity of time* (as much as space) in psychic (as much as physical) facts. For example, "A" dreams of a friend who has been dead for a few years and, the next day, with no warning, "B" seeks them to deliver a mediumistic message from the deceased, addressed to them. There, there are two phenomena: the mediumistic, which produces the message (not analyzing if the current purpose is truthful or not), and the *synchronic*, identifiable in the context of coincidence between the dream and the delivery of the message, precisely that of the deceased. Between one fact and the other (dream and message), there is no explicit causality, although it can be inferred.

One can divide Synchronic phenomena into three large groups:

> 1 The coincidence of a psychic state in the observer with a simultaneous, objective, external event that corresponds to the psychic state or content (e.g., the scarab), where there is no evidence of a causal connection between the psychic state and the external event, and where, considering the psychic relativity of space and time, such a connection is not even conceivable; 2 The coincidence of a psychic state with a corresponding (more or less simultaneous) external event taking place outside the observer's field of perception, i.e. at a distance, and only verifiable afterward; 3 The coincidence of a psychic state with a corresponding, a not yet existent future event that is distant in time and can likewise only be verified afterward (JUNG, 2005, par. 974).

Apparently, the events to which the theory of synchronicity apply are limited, not covering the complex range of mediumistic phenomena. However, the concept of synchronicity can be better suited in epistemological phenomena subordinated to parapsychology. This theory does not *explain*, nor does it seek to explain, the mechanisms of production of such phenomena. It only emphasizes its seemingly non-causal character. I assure that because attributing such events to properties of the unconscious places us before a *tautology*, a vicious circle of naming an unknown principle as the provider of a just as unknown phenomenon. In fact, one could say that it is only a name for certain events, and not a *theory* itself, as many want to believe.

Jung conceptualizes nature as a meeting of four main principles: energy, indestructible and present in all phenomena, the space-time continuum, the principle of causality, which establishes a constant connection between the two and the principle of *synchronicity*, which generates an *inconstant connection through contingency or "signification"*. In other words, the complex of nature is made out of a physical reality (the macrocosm), where causality prevails *almost* permanently, and of a psychic substrate, which can interfere in the *causal world*, generating *non-causal* phenomena. The non-causal phenomena would be produced by the *archetypes*, and Jung thus refers to this problem:

> These are indefinite, that is to say, they can be known and determined only approximately. Although associated with casual processes, of "carried" but them, they continually go beyond their frame of reference, an infringement to which I would give the name "transgressivity" because the archetypes are not found exclusively in the psychic sphere, but can occur just as much in circumstances that are not psychic (equivalence of an outward physical process with a psychic one). Archetypal equivalences are contingent on causal determination, that is to

say, there exist between them and the causal processes no relations that conform to law (JUNG, 2005, pp. 954).

According to Jung, the principle of synchronicity was a methodological requirement to explain the intrusion of psychic phenomena in a non-causal way, in the world governed by causality. Deep down, the inside out of the world is under the direction of the *archetypes*, entities of the *collective unconscious*, unable of been explained by experience, but accessible in their mythological or geometric projections, found in the magical-religious cultural structures of all peoples.

In 1857, long before Jung's birth, explanations of the so-called synchronic phenomena emerged, in addition to others not covered by the theory. According to this theory, the occurrence of an idea in several places at the same time, for example, a discovery such as the infinitesimal calculation by Newton and Leibniz, is due to the fact that the spirits are outside the body, during sleep, and exchange information that is retained in the unconscious, then appearing in consciousness as intuition. This theory, which implies the dissociation of the mind, has variants, such as the one that tells us that during sleep there is interaction between the spirits of the *living* among themselves, just as with the *dead*, which can facilitate the dissemination of similar ideas in various places, simultaneously (KARDEC, 2007, question 419).

Similarly, the theory in question explains that there is *unconscious communication* between individuals because the mind is not a prisoner of the body, like a liquid in a bottle. In fact, thoughts radiate through the environment as the light from the filament of an electric light bulb passes through the glass where it is contained. This allows subliminal communication between individuals in a permanent exchange of information. The sympathetic affinity between people allows such communication to occur instantly on certain occasions (KARDEC, 2007, questions 420- 421).

Therefore, the *spiritist hypothesis* is much simpler than those invented by the researchers of paranormal phenomena. The so-called hypothesis was launched by the phenomenon itself, or rather, by the spirits that communicate through mediumship, while the others were created by researchers, as opposed to what was stated by the phenomenon itself. Thus, while the spiritist hypothesis is *natural*, the researchers' one is *artificial*. Two renowned scholars of *psychic phenomena*, Gustav Geley and Charles Richet concluded that the hypothesis, although it is the simplest one, is the only that covers a wider range of phenomena, with no exception, while the others apply to limited types of paranormal phenomena. These are *retail theories*, which end up contradicting each other, and end up losing their effectiveness since so limited. Jung himself came to a similar conclusion (see JUNG, 2002, p. 85).

The *theory of synchronicity* has the value of showing that there are phenomena where the relationship between cause and effect, whether present or not, is recognizable. These phenomena are still requiring an explanatory hypothesis. Here is an example, taken from Jung's own clinic. One of his patients, with a strong Cartesian mentality, had been inaccessible to the psychological approach. Having tried to break this rationalist heart, Jung decided to wait for something unexpected to provide means of breaking into the psychic defenses of the patient:

> Well, I was sitting opposite her one day, with my back to the window, listening to her flow of rhetoric. She had an impressive dream the night before, in which someone had given her a gold scarab -- a costly piece of jewelry. While she was still telling me this dream, I heard something behind me gently tapping on the window. I turned around and saw that it was a fairly large flying insect that was knocking against the window from outside in an obvious effort to get into the dark room. This seemed to me very strange. I opened the window immediately and caught the insect in the air as it flew in. It was a scarabaeid beetle, or common rose-chafer (Cetonia aurata), whose gold-green color most nearly resembles that of a golden scarab. I handed the beetle to my patient with the words, "Here is your scarab". This experience punctured the desired hole in her rationalism and broke the ice of her intellectual resistance (JUNG, 2005, par. 842).

How to comprehend such a case? There is a coincidence between the dream and the appearance of the beetle, without a shadow of doubt. Was it a symbolic pre-cognition? That is, the patient saw, in her dream, that a beetle would try to enter the room, the next day, at the time of her appointment? It is a possible theory because as Jung teaches, the human psyche is beyond the space-time continuum. On the other hand, would the unconscious psyche have attracted the beetle to the point of leading it into a dark room, which is contrary to the general procedure of insects, since they are attracted by light? It is another possibility, since the beetle, like all living beings, has an unconscious structure, in its monad (spiritual protoform).

One could also argue that, when listening to the dream, Jung's unconscious attracted a beetle that resembled the scarab to continue the treatment! Another plausible hypothesis, according to analytical psychology.

Finally, would a *spiritual entity* have interfered, interested in therapeutic work with the patient, acting upon the beetle, causing it to crash into the glass, so that *synchronicity* would be evident? It cannot be discarded, as long as it is known that disembodied spirits are interested in those who have remained and meddle into their lives, for the most varied purposes.

It is a difficult choice, as all hypotheses are logically possible. Nevertheless, there are certain events, which we cannot yet determine the means of how they transpired. As an example, here is my own story: I was living in Ilhéus, a country town in the state of Bahia, Brazil, and I would travel to the city of Manaus, capital of the State of Amazonas, at 1:00 pm, making flight connections in Salvador and Brazilia. In the morning, at my office, I met two young women, who had reported me facts from their early childhood, including when they were newborns. Each of them, at different times, showed an intense *affection* while telling me their stories. I was stunned by the facts narrated. Both, though well married, were intensely opposed to having children. The conversation with the last one took place at twelve o'clock in the afternoon, and I had to quickly go to the house where I lived to get my suitcase and then run straight to the airport. The attendant of the aviation company had placed me in the middle seat, in the first row, on all three airplanes I would have to travel. I asked her to change my seat, joking with her: "My friend, I do not like to play the role of the sausage in a hot dog". She then placed me in the window seat, of the same first row, on the following flights, but the place on the first flight, which would take off half an hour later, remained the same. Upon boarding the plane, there was a young woman, with a child in her arms, in my seat. She then moved to a place by the window, and I sat on the place that had been previously assigned to me. In Salvador, I switched airplanes. But, to my surprise, on the seat by the window – where I would sit –, there was a lady, with a child in her arms. That reminded me of the morning reports and of what had happened on the first airplane. The connection in Brazilia took about two hours. When I boarded the plane that would take me to Manaus, another surprise: in the place by the window stood a young woman holding a child on her arms. During the conversation, she asked me where I would be staying, because she owned a hotel, named Da Vinci, and would make me a great price on the daily fee. I told her that I did not know because the friends who had invited me were arranging the lodging, which could even be in the residence of one of them. Finally, upon arrival, I learned that the companions had booked me a room at the Da Vinci Hotel.

As it turns out, a series of *coincidences*. What would have motivated them? Was there some connection between the morning events and the events on the planes? But what had provoked them? There is no point in seeking a solution in an act of spirits because there are not enough reasons to justify such an effort. This is a typical case of *synchronicity*, as established by Jung, but characterizing it does not explain it. What mechanisms caused these *coincidences*? Did my unconscious provoke all these encounters? Would the dialogues have affected it so much, that it made me cause the phenomenon of women with newborn children sitting in my seats? One thing is for sure, my seats had been booked in advance and without my knowledge, all three middle seats, and two of them were switched with no warning. Everything indicates that, with the exception of the first seat, which had not changed, the other two, next to the window, were booked, probably, after my reservations. I say probably because I do not know. And what is the point of knowing? The origins of the young women's problems, which I had attended to, were very clear! The collection of synchronicities did not bring me any clarification, except assuring that my conclusions were correct.

Origin and Evolution of Spirits

Spirits, like everything else that exists, are created by God. We read in *The Spirits' Book*:

> Did spirits have a beginning or have they existed from all eternity like God?
> If spirits had no beginning, they would be equal to God; on the contrary, they are God's creation and subject to the divine will. God has existed from all eternity – that is incontestable – but we know nothing as to when and how we spirits were created. You could say that we had no beginning if you mean that since God is eternal, then God must have always and unceasingly created spirits. Nevertheless, when and how each of us was created individually, I will repeat: no one knows. It is a mystery. (KARDEC, 2007, question 78).

Man, however, never conforms to limits and difficulties in the process of knowledge, let alone with mysteries, interpreting them as challenges to be accepted and solved. Therefore, thinkers have been trying to penetrate the secrets of creation in general and, in particular, the ones related to the creation of spirits. Regarding the *when* of creation, we learn once more what we have already studied before: the impossibility of defining a time frame, for events that took place at the moment time was created. Still, if we follow Ubaldi's thought and his monism, we will be able to see the matter as an element to evolve into spirit.

Among contemporary thinkers, Jean E. Charon proposes that the spirit is the electron itself, i.e., that each electron contains the whole set of information that shapes the spirit. It would be a mini black hole possessing the negentropic ability to store an increasing volume of information, achieved by the exchange of information with other electrons, through the exchange of virtual photons. The electron would have intelligence and volition. The weak point of the theory is that the spirit could not present the psychological unity that would characterize it, except for a miraculous instant informational update mechanism.

The Brazilian Dr. Hernani Guimarães Andrade (1913-2003), around 1959, launched his Corpuscular Theory of the Spiritism, similar to the Corpuscular theory of Matter, launched in 1803 by Dalton in England. He studies the evidence presented by the mediumistic manifestations and stated that many spiritist and biological phenomena reveal their vibratory nature. A large majority leads to the conclusion that the key to explaining the spirit's rule over matter, and its reaction over matter, lies in the mutual actions between two fields: the biomagnetic and the electromagnetic. Admitting the spirit as a continuum, several difficulties are manifested for the sake of explaining these and the other observed facts. When one reaches the domains of vibratory manifestations, such as luminous apparitions, then the difficulty becomes greater, because the elasticity of the emitting source becomes evident. If a substance is susceptible to vibrate, it will present denser parts and rarefied parts (ANDRADE, 1959, pp. 28). He also said that we must assume that the spiritual substance is susceptible to differentiation, since the spirits themselves declare it as being in fact (ANDRADE, 1959, pp. 29).

Andrade postulates the existence of spirit particles, forming the spiritual atom, naming them: *intelecton*, with a quantum of intelligence; bion, with a quantum of life; and mentalton, with a quantum of perception. In the spiritual atom, the bion corresponds to the electron, with the same negative polarity and responsible for the formation of animal electricity or animal magnetism, as well as the biomagnetic fields, fortifier of organic matter; the *mentalton* would correspond to the neutron, with the same electrical neutrality and conjugating with the *intelecton*, of positive charge, to form the nucleus. A spiritual atom, composed of a *bion* that circulates the nucleus formed by a mentalton plus an *intelecton*, would correspond to the material hydrogen atom, and, as said by Dr. Hernani. Further on, he explains that this elemental spiritual atom, having its *Biomagnetic* field annulled due to the bion's movement in a four-dimensional wrapper, keeps a neutral balance outside the physical space, or rather, has its natural habitat within the hyperspace. Animating a living being — the most elementary conceivable – the Biomagnetic field of the *Monad* represents the prototype of the soul (ANDRADE, 1959, pp. 43-44).

In the 1986 book *Quantum Psi*, where he updates his thesis of 59, Andrade calls the spiritual atom a *psi-Atom* and the *mentalton*, *perception*, in accordance with its functions. He also applies modern concepts of quantum physics to his own theory. In his opinion, Dr. *Hernani's* theory is very elucidative and explains a number of phenomena linked to spiritist life and facts. However, it is a long way from that point until making the spirit, as an intelligent principle, a conglomerate of particles. He feels that the Corpuscular theory, or its new quantum version, describes phenomena of the immediate spiritual world, as well as applies to the psychosome, a manifestation organism of the spirit at this cosmic level.

In *The Spirits' Book*, the following statement is found: *Hence, everything is useful; everything in nature is linked together, from the primitive atom to the archangel, who also began as only an atom – an admirable law of harmony, which your limited minds cannot yet grasp in its entirety* (KARDEC, 2007, question 540).

This statement allows us to meditate on the object of the current study. If the archangel began as an atom, we must consider the spirit as a result of an evolution of matter, which it seems to us as an indication of a monistic way of analyzing the problem, and a principle of clarification on the broad lines of the creative process. Naturally not answering all questions that may arise. Allan Kardec thus expressed himself on the subject:

> Whether they have a common origin and necessary points of contact between them, and whether intelligence has its own independent existence or is only a property or effect, as some claim, or even whether it is an emanation of the Divinity this is all unknown to us. Matter and intelligence are distinct, as far as we are concerned; thus, we regard them as the two constituent principles of the universe. Above all, we see an intelligence that dominates all others, that governs all of them, that distinguishes itself from them by essential attributes: it is this supreme intelligence that we call God (KARDEC, 2007, Kardec's comment to question 28).

As you can see, question 540 established an initial response to the consolidator's reasoning, creating an evolutionary bond between the perfect spirit and matter. This precedes the model outlined in *The Great Synthesis* in about 76 years. In this work, edited for the first time in Brazil by the Brazilian Spiritist Federation, in the pages of *The Reformer*, in 1933, is proposed the emergence of the spirit from matter. Ubaldi's Monism flows into the most complete pantheism, making everything a result of the Divine substance, which would ultimately be the forming energy of all that exists. However, we cannot agree (although we respect his right to postulate and defend the philosophical and religious views he has built), in the Ubaldi model, with the thesis of the fallen Angels, which is but a throwback to the outdated elucubrations of medieval thinkers, and seems to hurt logic, common sense and, what is more serious, the very concept that we have of God.

Undoubtedly, the proposition of a vast evolutionary process from a fundamental energy, the Universal fluid, to the Pure Spirit, is of a very great intellectual seduction, because it draws a concept of God so immense that we are spontaneously led to praise and prayer. The revelation's statement about God as the Alpha and the Omega, Beginning and End, Departure and Arrival of the immense Cosmic Drama.

An evolutionary view that separates Matter and Spirit makes no sense. It goes against what contemporary Science unravels: the empire of energy. Energy condenses itself in particles, forming the atom, which, in turn, interacts with others, constituting the molecules – consequently, all things and beings that we know. Matter is frozen energy, Einstein has established. And in an energetic Cosmos, The Spirit must be included, as a specific type of energy, possibly an evolution of this one. Thus, everything will be integrated into an indissoluble totality, in a continuous chain, completing a harmonious picture of the whole Creation.

9. Earth's Spiritual Counterpart: theoretical essay

Considering the spiritual descriptions about the Earth, our planet, like the other celestial bodies, has a counterpart formed by the matter of the *Spiritual Universe*, or astral. Its conformation is basically the same of our planet, respecting the proportions. It presents a geomorphology similar to the terrestrial orb: mountain ranges, valleys, plains, gorges and canyons, rivers, lakes, swamps, seas and oceans, diverse flora, included the forests, *caatingas*, sandbanks, flowers and fruit trees, as well as a diverse fauna, formed by animals proper to that place, ranging from insects to giant saurians, countless reptiles, birds of innumerous species, just as unknown to us as to the spirits of terrestrial animals there take some time in between reincarnations.

It also presents weather phenomena, from mild breezes to fearsome hurricanes, from small atmospheric variations up to powerful storms, with tremendous electric discharges, in addition to seismic shocks such as earthquakes, tidal waves and volcanoes, throughout the range we know. In the *Spiritual Land*, we also find Continents, Islands, Peninsulas, and the whole range of geographic features that we know, as well as peoples of various ethnicities and degrees of civilization: from primitive to civilized, from uncultured to technologically developed, and/or spiritually, from Warriors to saints and peacemakers. The social structures present all the variations that humanity has known throughout its history. Among the majority of the groups, there are wars of conquest and, therefore, one is able to find empires and the many forms of domination we have experienced throughout our development. Countless religious beliefs, from primitive rituals to demonic cults and black magic, to traditional religions, are spread throughout the astral ecumenism, in continuation to the individual and collective preferences, taken from the Earth, as well as cultural and religious postures born from its own conditions.

Its constant wars impose a continuous migratory flow between the continents of the astral globe. The economy of undeveloped groups is based on the exploitation of animal, plant, mineral and others energetic resources, and the vital fluid is the most important product, extracted from living beings, particularly from humans, on a large scale, with the purpose of maintaining the physical sensations, appetites and animal impulses. Commercial and industrial paraphernalia is structured around the collection of vital energy, sustained by an immense exploitation apparatus, formed by technicians equipped with sophisticated techniques.

On the other hand, an innumerable contingent of spirits awakening to the greater realities of Life is distributed throughout the spiritual and physical world, in functions of neutralizing the activities of groups that cultivate unbalanced, diverse passions. They perform a systematic effort aimed at improving the psychic level of Souls, promoting a radical change in the guidelines and structures of spiritual societies based on selfishness and its derivatives: pride, vanity, lasciviousness, lust, perversity, violence, etc.

The *spiritual counterpart of the Earth* must have been structured because of the influence of the planet's electromagnetic and gravitational field, since its formation. The planetary mass, acting upon the interdimensional frontier, must have caused astral matter to condense, remaining linked by gravitational and electromagnetic interaction, developed by both masses, in the process of transdimensional interaction, in a game of transcendent actions and high-power reactions.

The *Spiritual Earth* has probably developed in the immense field generated by the condensation of the material that gave rise to the Sun and its planetary procession, which leads us to conclude there is an Astral Planetarium System, juxtaposed and interacting with our Solar System, because the large mass concentrations, both in one dimension and in the other, should cause induction reactions. It can also be inferred that such an action between the two dimensions will happen in the opposite direction, that is, from the *Spiritual Universe* to the *Material Universe*, causing the appearance of diverse bodies and astronomical phenomena.

Antiquity of the Concept of Spiritual Land

All primitive peoples, both of antiquity and today, have conceived the spiritual region as being similar to Earth. They divide it between a region of suffering and another of happiness and joy.

When the Neanderthals began to bury the dead, they demonstrated a philosophy about life in the afterlife, as we can see from the way they proceeded in the burial. Funeral ceremonies are universal and as old as man is. From the first known remains, up to the present day, the tomb has been the most basic religious expression, and it is one of the most evident proof of the belief in a life hereafter, with the same substance of the human being, even the tribes of less developed religious mentality, until current primitive peoples that profess and exhibit absolute atheism, for example, due to politics, that however, when honoring their dead, review the permanence of this basic idea, at times, distorted, that can only be explained by the belief in the existence beyond the grave (CID & RIU, 1965, pp. 11).

The indigenous peoples of North America referred to the *Spiritual Earth* as a place where there was plenty of hunting, fishing, and where the products grown did not suffer the inclemency of time, producing with plenty. There they were guaranteed hunting pleasures and tournaments of bravery and strength, in disputes with other strong and manly warriors, glory and eternal satisfaction. Prehistoric man, like the later and present primitive, believe in the maintenance of personality in the afterlife, with needs very similar to earthly ones, as demonstrated by the weapons, adornments and food offered to the dead and found next to their remains, in the graves. The investigations have clarified that it is not the material objects, but their spirits, that accompany the dead, in the same way, that it is not the physical body of the deceased who survives in the afterlife, but its spectrum. Except for this transposition to a spectral plane, this existence is equal to the earthly one (CID & RIU, 1965, pp.11-12). The religious tradition of the Egyptians speaks, like almost all religions, of a *postmortem* trial, after which absolved souls would live in environments that copied the everyday life of the banks of the Nile, but without their difficulties and problems, where they could hunt, fish and have intense pleasures, in a climate of permanent euphoria and happiness. Moreover, the culprits would be transferred to places worse than the times of drought and famine, when there were no floods in the Nile alongside humus fertilizer, compounded by constant torments inflicted by a legion of infernal beings.

The Hindus, in their various religious currents, all united by common philosophical and theological principles, describe heavenly astral planets, subordinated to less powerful deities, where good souls, that had not yet found enlightenment, enjoy the joys of an abundant life, surrounded by fauna and flora and pleasant harmonious ambiance, feeling the happiness of those who have freed themselves from the unfortunate impulses. Others, tortured and full of dangers and painful obstacles, welcome souls who had lost themselves in subordination to instincts.

The religion of the Classical World describes the abode of the Gods on Mount Olympus as a portrait of an earthly society, where hatred, jealousy, adultery, struggles, intrigues, they all reign, and are magnified by the supernatural life, of magical powers, of its inhabitants. They eat, drink, sleep, in short, they are transcendent human beings. The dead live in a dark *Hades*, where there are rivers, caves, lakes, that is, geographical features and meteorological phenomena, to the point that the location of the world of shadows is described as being in the bowels of the Earth. There, too, would be found a twisted flora, but still composed of vegetables, in addition to a monstrous fauna, whose largest representative was Cerberus, the three-headed dog, Keeper of the portals of the Pluto's world. In it lived inhabitants like Charon, in whose boat the dead crossed the Styx, described as a hirsute and ferocious old man, who had to be paid with the coin that was placed in the mouth of the corpses before they were buried. Contrary to this gloomy place, the *Elysium* and the *Isle of the Blessed*, and other pleasant corners, welcomed the souls of the elect, fair and heroes, where a gentle nature, rich in fruits, beautiful and docile animals, allowed them to enjoy a life of peace and joy, in an eternal and stable happiness.

The Barbarian peoples, like The Primitives, conceived a perspective of materiality. The dead warriors, valiantly killed in combat, received the gift of an eternal life of fights and tournaments, embraced by beautiful and valiant women, who provided them with pleasure. The cowards and treacherous received the punishment deserved in places of pain, of anguish.

In Christianity, Jesus teaches that: *In my Father's house are many rooms; if it were not so, I would have told you; for I go to prepare a place for you* (John 14: 2). The term *rooms* express the idea of specific locations. The New Testament refers to *throne of God*, and *Crystal Lake, Thrones of elders, books, trumpets, robes, golden altar, temple, bowls, horses, chains, swords, keys, lakes of fire and brimstone*, and even a whole city: *The New Jerusalem*. A series of analogies, which demonstrate an intuition, if not a knowledge rather fragmentary and distorted about spirituality.

Islamism, whose origins are interwoven with mosaicism and Coptic Christianity, materializes certain aspects of heaven, placing in it the Huris, beautiful and sensual women, for the joy of the righteous, as, equally, a hell of physical and moral pains for punishment of the wicked.

The Spiritual World in Mediumistic Communications

Long before the Fox sisters, in the mid-eighteenth century, Emmanuel Swedenborg, Swedish of culture and polymorphic skills, had a fantastic mediumistic blossoming, which made him experience interesting spiritual facts. He described the beyond as formed by various spheres, distributed by degrees of evolution and spirits' improvement. His descriptions speak of houses, where families live, temples, auditoriums and palaces. Finally, real cities with political-administrative direction, social life, etc. There are weddings, crafts, music, literature, flowers and fruits, gardens and orchards, science, schools, museums, gyms, libraries and sport. That is, the disembodied, especially when still very close to the physical emotions, habits and customs of the life they have abandoned, only with the aspect of realizing everything within a constant effort to experience virtues and moral nobility. On the other hand, he points out communities of pain and suffering, formed by spirits that lived the demeaning and petty instincts, addictions and defects on Earth.

With the Hydesville phenomena, mediumship became known in the USA and then in the rest of the world. The most remarkable thing in early spiritist Communications is that, despite the mediums belonging to the so-called Christian religions, they described the spiritual life in complete disagreement with the religious education of the mediators, as well as that which they had cherished while incarnate. They rule out the existence of the devil and an eternal heaven and hell, with an infernal court. Opposed to the Theory of Grace (on the subject see ARGOLLO, 1992, Chapter VII), they assign to each one the responsibility for the type of life faced in the Beyond. The generality of the descriptions of cities draws the attention, with intense social life, in the spiritual regions, landscapes with rivers, lakes, mountains, forests, orchards, gardens, animals and birds of a varied type. Family life, engagement, marriage, learning of numerous courses. An entire ecosystem similar to the terrain, keeping, however, fundamental differences, because all things can be done instantly, thanks to the ideoplasticity of spiritual matter, perceptions and sensations are activated to a maximum degree, as they also have specific characteristics of the fourth dimension where they are given. Thus, for example, the view is not limited to the relative perspective of the object, but from all angles at the same time, and the hearing is replaced with telepathic, instantaneous and global capture, etc. As the means reflect the mentality of the spirits that live in them, and these are grouped by moral affinity, there are happy and unhappy locations.

For a clearer idea of the subject, I recommend reading *The Crisis of Death*, by Ernesto Bozzano, where one can find many messages in which the disembodied describe ways and processes of their death, as well as the similarity of the spiritual habitat with the terrestrial in some passages.

It is interesting to note that the NDE (Near Death Experiences), in which people who were on the threshold of death and were resurrected by doctors describe places and people they visited, during the seconds they remained dead, are similar to the messages analyzed by Bozzano, which works as additional evidence for both studies.

Dr. Raymond A. Moody Jr., in *Life After Life* – a book that has already been read by millions of people, throughout the world –, studies facts of NDE that occurred in the United States and investigated by him. Common description: passage through a tunnel, which shows luminosity in its other extreme. After crossing the tunnel, the person emerged in a garden, whose flowers present luminosity, in addition to colorful variety. Meeting with relatives and already disembodied friends, who present themselves rejuvenated and enjoying good health, no longer suffering, nor from old age or the diseases that victimized them. The meeting with the Spiritual guide, whose affection and kindness stimulates and regenerates the interlocutor.

All these facts are similar to those described in the book of the Italian spiritist philosopher, worth comparing both works.

As seen, the NDE occurred, most times, with people that had been distanced from religious concerns, or linked to traditional beliefs, confirming the existence of environments similar to those of the Earth, in the spiritual dimension.

The communications received through electronic equipment, well known in Europe today – mainly in the Germanic regions –, prove the materiality of Near-Earth spirituality. Jüergenson, who systematically initiated this way of communication with spirits in the last century, received information about the existence of environments similar to those of the Earth.

These mediumistic experiences, sophisticated by the use of modern electromagnetic techniques, illustrate the truth of the spiritist messages, received at all times, on this and other subjects (for more details, see ARGOLLO, 1994).

I could use other circumstantial evidence to corroborate what I have addressed at the beginning of this chapter, but I prefer to stop here, letting the readers search for themselves, which will lead them not only to remarkable discoveries but to the personal certainty about immortality and the continuity of life in a dimension where, inexorably, each one will live a pleasant or unpleasant situation, according to the cultivated inner life during the incarnation. All of this will also serve the purpose to demonstrate that Jesus' teachings in the Gospels are not mere rhetorical figures, nor superficial moralism, but scientific axioms, the application or lack of which will reflect on each of us, producing good or bad effects, joy or suffering.

Physical **Conditions of the Spiritual Land**

According to the spirits that communicate through the mediums, the striking feature of the *Spiritual Land* is the distribution of its inhabitants by *vibratory levels* and *affinity patterns*, which leads to the creation of narrow social groups closed within themselves. Moreover, due to the peculiarities of the environment and the Psychosomatics reflecting and externalizing the inclinations of individuals, in addition to the ease of telepathic apprehension of feelings and thoughts, spiritual societies, such as *Our Home*, and others of the same level, are more repressive than earthly societies, where the individual has privacy in relation to their fellow men.

Thus, it is explained why the spirit needs to reincarnate: in the spiritual environment, each one gravitates towards the group that is related to them, where they start to reinforce feelings and group ideas while suffering the pressure of the same group upon themselves. In a place like *Our Home*, it is impossible to hide a thought and/or feeling, because the majority, at least, will be perceiving it. It is not possible to think negatively, that is, contrary to the dominant ethics, because thought projects itself in the environment, and in the spirit itself, in specific phenomena, becoming blatant to those around them. Obligated to maintain a pattern of thought and behavior consistent with what they were used to when incarnated, there is no way of knowing whether the moral evolution that the spirit presents is the result of *voluntary evolution*, by acceptance of ethical postulates, or the result of pressure from the environment. In the case of unhappy spiritual communities, lower feelings will tend to be exacerbated by the sum of negative impulses and thoughts.

The spirit André Luiz, through Francisco Cândido XAVIER, says that in adapting to the continents of the extraphysical sphere, the consciousness that had learned to perform complex transubstantiations of force in the various lines of nature begins to maneuver alongside the phenomena of mentation and reflection, that thought is the fundamental basis (XAVIER, 1985, p. 93).

Surely, in the new action sphere, to which one sees themself taken by death, they find matter known in the world, on a new scale. More complicated and subtle atomic elements, beyond hydrogen and uranium, in a different form from that in which they are characterized in the planetary gleba, magnify the stoichiogenetic series. The soil of the spiritual world, structured with similar resources, all of them rising in the quintessence, correspond to the specific weight of the spirit, and, holding virtual possibilities and richness, await for them in order to be populated with glory and beauty (XAVIER, 1985, p. 96).

In the dwelling of continuity to which they are transferred, men find, therefore, the same laws of gravitation that control the Earth, with the days and nights marking the account of time, although the severity of the seasons is suppressed by environmental factors that ensure the harmony of nature. Plants and animals domesticated by human intelligence, for millennia, can be acclimatized and improved there, for certain periods of existence, at the end of which they return to their nucleus of origin in the Earth's soil, to advance in the evolutionary pilgrimage (XAVIER, 1985, p. 96-97).

Moral Gravity in the Spirit World

Many communicating spirits have stated, in different countries and eras, that the immediate plan for men's residence lies subdivided into several spheres. This is not the case from space's point of view, but rather from the point of view of conditions, which occurs on the globe of denser matter, where man steps proudly.

Just as on Earth, all beings are subjected to the *law of gravity*, those of the *Spiritual Earth* are subject to a similar law, the *law of moral gravity*, which says that by virtue of the specific weight of feelings and dominant thoughts in the spirits, they are attracted to the level of the corresponding reality. And, along these vast regions of subtle matter that surround the cyclopean body of the planet, with major cavity zones, under the lines that mark the beginning of exploitation, as seen in the crust of the Earth itself, extending from the continental surface to the bed of the oceans, the happy and less happy settlements begin, as well as the Infernal agglomerations of disembodied creatures who, fearing the forms of their own thoughts, take refuge in the shadows, and detest light (XAVIER, 1985, p. 96).

The Evolution of Earth's Spiritual Counterpart

Obviously, the spiritual part of the Earth, or the *psi-Earth*, as Hernani Guimarães Andrade calls it, has evolved alongside its physical part.

In the early times of the planet, it must have shown diffuse and seismic phenomena, as in primitive Earth. The energetic elements of the spiritual environment, attracted by the fields formed by the planetary body, were shaped to electromagnetic influences, related to Earth's own structure, distributing themselves in its dimensional vicinities, probably as filings upon magnets, in the physical experience.

The emergence of life on Earth must have been predicted by the development of *monads* or *spirit elements*, according to Dr. Hernani's theory. Which means the appearance of life in the surrounding spiritual dimension, because, as explained above, it has flora and fauna besides spirits of higher animals. Here is a new field to be studied by scientists of the future: the appearance of life on the Spiritual Earth, as well as its evolutionary development. Did it follow the same principles of material nature? For this, it would be necessary the existence of a *natural selection* process, where the law of destruction would have full validity. This would imply a game of life and death, with the survival of the fittest. The spiritual fauna and flora would have to be outside the existential human, which characterizes the human spirit.

As it turns out, the spiritist revelations about the spiritual world raise a number of interesting questions. Would the spiritual animals and plants be a creation of the spirits' unconscious, incarnate and disembodied? Would they have been formed in the same way as the houses, cities, clothes and other equipment elaborated by the representation of the disembodied? We do not yet have a position on the subject, which requires research and meditation.

The action of the biomagnetic fields of elements-spirits, which would have led to the appearance of the replicating molecules on primitive Earth. The dialectical counteraction of the most primitive forms of earthly life, under the law of *Natural Selection*, through their spiritual herds or *proto-spirits*, may have led to modifications in these proto-spirits which, in turn, have generated an evolution by the aggregation of new spiritual principles and molecules.

The contiguous spiritual sphere, before the appearance of the human being with their processes of ideation and continuous thinking, should reflect the *fragmentary impulses* of animal minds, in their various stages of evolution, which should translate, from my point of view, into a game of changes, in perpetual motion, and fantastic elaborations, similar to the artistic productions of abstractionism.

Following parallel paths, in permanent dialectical Interaction, spirit and organism started to merge, according to the models already raised by Biology, through its numerous researchers of yore and from today. It should also be taken into account the activity of the spirits responsible for the Earth, who have always acted on both planes, changing and correcting things whenever necessary. Even, putting to ending useless genetic experiments, aimed at creating a *basic human organism*.

As the human being appeared, that is, when the spirit reached self-awareness, the spiritual world began to reflect on another subject, because on the contrary of animals whose spirits should not pass through a long erraticity, the disembodied human spirit takes some time in those regions and, thus, the mental projections of Incarnates and disembodied model their physical appearance. However, the morphological aspect of the immediate spiritual zone on Earth continued to reflect the limited mental processes of prehistoric man.

Immigrant spirits, as explained by Kardec in Chapter XI of *Genesis* and Emmanuel, by Francisco Candido XAVIER, in Chapter III of *On the way to the Light*, have transformed and defined the current structure of the earthly spiritual plane. Immigrants, as settlers who in fact they were, created advanced social structures, with cities and government, long before doing it on the physical plane, through the incarnation. There appeared the first advanced nucleus of civilization, which only much later came to be implanted among the incarnates. The *Law of Solidarity between inhabited worlds* provides the exchange of spiritual beings among planetary communities. In the same way, as between us, the "civilized" peoples settled in the continents discovered between the fifteenth and sixteenth centuries, transferring groups of individuals to the discovered regions and to the middle of the ethnic groups that existed there, intellectually evolved spirits are transferred to orbs with spirits in the primary phase of evolution, whose general vibration of violent passions coincide with the moral level of those. The already developed mental faculties of immigrants and their socio-cultural achievements accelerate the mental and social progress of the natives who, without the help, would spend vast intervals of time, counted to the millions, to attain the status of civilization. Prior to this providence, progress occurred through the direct influence of Earth's spiritual leaders who educated groups of disembodied men, through pedagogical processes of ideoplastic creations, stimulating the creative functions of primitive minds.

Thus, in general — in our way of thinking —, the evolution of the *Psychic Earth* was processed, in order to achieve the shape that we know today.

Final Synthesis

Upon analyzing planet Earth, one is placed before an astronomic body, where a large complex of physical, chemical and psychological phenomena occurs.

As in all the material universe, such phenomena happen on two levels: micro and macrocosmic. That is, the infinitely small and the immensely large. In general, the macrocosmic is a function of the microcosmic or otherwise:

$$Mac = F (Mic)$$

In the atomic kingdom, we see that there are also levels of derivation, such as: 1) molecular, 2) atomic 3) subatomic, or particles, including their structural components, or subparticles.

We can also say that the molecule is a function of the atom and that it belongs to the particles. This situation extends towards the infraparticles, which are formed of subparticles, such as quarks, and their diverse colors and flavors.

Between the atomic stratum and the macroscopic one finds a profound difference in the form of being. While the objects of our world behave according to certain laws that give them a character of sharpness and behavioral predictability, in the world of the atom events occur randomly, only being able to be studied by means of probabilistic criteria, that take away certainty. This concept of current science can, and should, be analyzed and discussed very carefully.

As for the scientific community, parapsychological studies are signaling what I have just affirmed, because they propose a challenge to the current scientific structure, working in phenomena that do not behave according to traditional axioms, considered immovable dogmas, definitive conquests of modern knowledge.

One of the dearest scientific dogmas is causality. It is true that Heisenberg and the Copenhagen School, facing the anger of the orthodox led by Einstein, had worked with proposals of non-causal phenomena in the atomic universe, however, it was the scholars of paranormal facts who first challenged the *status quo* by making experiments that did not fit into the causalistic schemes and, what is worse, undermined the foundations of the energy conservation dogma, an unthinkable heresy.

Despite the rejection of the conservatives, traditional science approaches the conclusions of psychic research, currently advocated under the name of Parapsychology, through its physical aspect. Quantum mechanics is demolishing entrenched philosophical positions, as Einsteinian relativity overthrew the traditional view of absolute time and space. Objectivity's overthrow in the phenomenal world leads us to the ancient Hindu concept of Maya, that is, the physical structures as a mere illusion, a dream, with no real existence. In this web of appearances, the spirit is trapped and forced to live countless pseudo-situations in a fantastic kaleidoscope of fantasies. The consolidating spirits have corroborated this thesis in *The Spirits' Book* when they state that our perception of the world originates from the organic structure that the human being has (questions 30 and following).

The studies on mediumistic and psychic phenomena reveal new means of perception, which we were not, in general, using in a conscious way, such as we do with the usual senses.

> The study of psychical sciences is the most important one in which you can engage today. The new instrument of investigation that you should develop and that has been developing naturally is precisely your latent consciousness. You have looked long enough outside yourselves; you should now solve the problem of your own selves and you will have thereby solved all the other problems. Gradually accustom your mind to following this new order of ideas. If you are able to transfer the center of your personality onto these deeper strata, you will notice new senses to arise in you, an animistic perception, a faculty of direct vision, which is that intuition I have spoken. Purify yourselves morally; refine the sensitiveness of the instrument that is yourselves and only then you will be able to see (Ubaldi, 1959, pp. 19).

Here is a summary of the researcher's results, which impose new problems, opening up perspectives of expansion for our knowledge on the real dimension of human perception. The phenomena present the characteristic of occurring as if time and space did not exist. The first experiments, right after the events of 1848 with the Fox sisters, led to the fact that they happened instantly, no matter how far the mediums or psychics were. For example, a spiritual entity could communicate simultaneously through two mediums, at the same time, and in places as far away as possible. It was not possible to measure time difference between the two phenomena. Nowadays the fact is even more evident, when we see its occurrence, by simultaneous communications of an entity through several mediators, at the same time and in different locations. A broader survey on the subject is needed, one that questions our ideas about space and time, which naturally occur differently for spirits.

In the telepathic phenomenon, the space-time problem arises ostensibly, being the most important problem for parapsychologists and congeners. Whatever the distance between the transmitter and the receiver, even if one is on the hidden side of the moon, and the other on Earth, such as it has already been checked. Experiments with clairvoyance raise the question of the structure of space, since it also happens immediately, no matter how far the object is from perception, and the same reasoning can be extended to the facts of clairvoyance. Similarly, studies on the transport of objects to, and from, closed places, even if these objects are on the other side of the Earth. In this case, penetration of matter by the matter is presented, a common thing in the phenomena of physical effects and from which studies Zöllner drew the conviction of a fourth dimension, habitat of the disincarnated spirits.

One thing that stands out from spiritist studies is its similarity with events registered by the quantum studies. From the tunnel effect to the Einstein-Podolsky-Rosen paradox, from particles that move back in time (as is also the case with psychometry, or vision of past events, from contact with objects) to the intervention of the mind of the experimenter directing the experience to a result that he desires, there are so many similarities that one can step away from the concept of coincidence. It was because of this that Jung associated himself with the physicist Wolfgang Pauli, creating the theory of synchronicity, seeking to explain the aspect of non-causality of paranormal or mediumistic phenomena. The mediumistic facts reveal a wealth of perceptions that, although they happen often, have not been used by us in all fullness, and they can open up new dimensions to human progress. They give amplitude to Bergson's postulations on intuition, in addition to providing us with the means to broaden our knowledge of all that exists in the world, as well as what does not yet exist for us.

Seeing the past, registering the future, capturing images from a distance, making objects cross material obstacles, projecting thought from a distance, or recording it in photographic film, those are phenomena that modify our scientific view of the world, giving rise to a review of the concepts of the universe, in all knowledge areas.

Above all, however, are the phenomena of communication between the living and the dead, because they introduce the fact of personal immortality, which by itself is the greatest revolution in the history of human evolution. In addition, the finding on the truthfulness of what religions have affirmed since immemorial centuries.

One answers the eternal question of philosophers about life and death, although so much of the existence is still questionable, and needs to be answered because what is said until now, even in the Spiritist sphere, does not answer it in reality, because it depends on the will of God.

The discovery of the spirit allows the uncovering of the spiritual world, about which we have already had the opportunity to express ourselves, pages ago.

The process of knowledge goes beyond, in definition, sensual and idealistic propositions, with the realization of spiritual senses as active means of knowledge, overlapping the narrow limits of the physical, traditional senses.

Knowledge involves not only the nervous system, which has in the brain the center coordinates and processor, but the entire perispiritual complex, where the millions of sensory stimuli are integrated and elaborated, all under the spirit's orders (intelligent principle), which manages the process as a whole. Naturally, as it happens with the nervous system, all perispirit energy levels have automatic processing and reflex reaction devices that ask for immediate response. Similarly, the conscious structures of perception do not remain only linked to the structures of the unconscious, with its archetypes, according to Jungian studies, but to an unconscious that guards all the experiences of being, through the palingenetic process, besides being enlightened by the lights of the future unconscious, or superconscious, seat of altruistic, artistic impulses, etc. Memory, having the records of past lives, expands the integration of knowledge, leading to a new theory of learning thus, with no further doubt, learning is remembering, as Socrates had already intuited.

Speaking of intuition, this is a faculty that will have to be much more used, in the future, to the extent that men improve spiritually. We can and must employ, intuition at all times of our lives, which will provide us with more safety in acts and deliberations. About this faculty and its development, writes the Spirit Emmanuel, through Francisco Cândido XAVIER, stating that it is necessary, in our times, that one seeks to develop all their spiritual energies -- hidden forces that await their desire to fully blossom. Men need their intuitive faculties through successive exercises of the mind, which, in turn, must vibrate to the rhythm of generous ideals. Each individuality should extend the circle of their spiritual skills, for, as a reward for their perseverance and effort, they will be able to be sure about the sublime truths of the invisible world, without the help of any intermediaries. What is necessary to them, however, is love, devotion, pure aspiration and unshakable faith, concentrated in this light that the heart fervently craves; this spiritual state will increase the vibratory power of the mind and man will then be born for a better life (XAVIER, 2003, pp. 49-50).

Pietro Ubaldi conveys:

> Do not be frightened of this incomprehensible word: intuition. Begin by not denying it and it will emerge to you. Evolution, that great concept that science has affirmed (although incompletely and with erroneous consequences), is not a chimera and impels your nervous system toward an increasingly refined sensitiveness, to which intuition is a prelude. In this way, this deeper psyche will manifest itself in you perforce of the natural law of evolution via a fatally approaching maturity. You will set aside, for the usage of practical life, that outward and superficial psyche of yours, which is reason, because only through this inward psyche, which is part of your innermost self, will you be able to understand the deeper reality latent in the depth of things. This is the only way leading to the knowledge of the Absolute. Only among similar beings is it possible to establish communication. And in order to understand the mystery existing in all things you must learn how to descend to the mystery lying within you. (Ubaldi, 1959, pp.18).

The ideas I have just outlined are intended to place some elucubrations regarding evolution, according to the Spiritist perspective. I hope that it can stimulate ideal companions who, disagreeing or agreeing with their principles, discuss them with the necessary depth and competence that I lack.

At no time do I position myself as the holder of truth, imposing concepts via *magister dixit*. Every day I am confronted by my ignorance in the face of the problems that Spiritism imposes on the intellectual thinking. All that was written in the previous pages has a speculative character, as I said at the beginning, therefore, suffers from the precariousness of any and all species. If one is able to show to me, logically, with substantial arguments, that these speculations are so wrong, I shall, in all good will, expose the point of view of whoever does it. However, I will not accept, under any hypothesis, the contradictory statement based on any pseudo-authority, from whoever does it, or from someone to whom one might turn. Allan Kardec taught me that Spiritism is freedom and common sense. As there is no decision-making authority in the spiritist movement, who can establish what should be thought or not — what is right or wrong — it is concluded that only persuasion, by clear and obvious reasoning, leads to either change of views.

Faced with the immensity that is the Spiritist doctrine – new knowledge, not yet sufficiently understood by those who profess its principles – we must study, meditate and learn, humbly bowing our bodies before God's greatness and wisdom, not forgetting at any time that, as Paul said: *knowledge swells, but love builds*.

Bibliographic Sources

ANDRADE, Hernani Guimarães. *A Teoria Corpuscular do Espírito.* 2ª. Edição. São Paulo-SP: Edição do autor, 1959.

AKSAKOF, Alexander. *Animismo ou Espiritismo* 2ª. Edição. Rio de Janeiro-RJ: Federação Espírita Brasileira, 1956.

ARGOLLO, Djalma Argollo. *O Novo Testamento: um enfoque espírita.* São Paulo-SP: Editora Mnêmio Túlio, 1992.

ARGOLLO, Djalma Argollo. *Espiritismo e Transcomunicação.* 2ª. Edição. São Paulo-SP: Editora Mnêmio Túlio,1994

ARGOLLO, Djalma Argollo. *Jung e a Mediunidade.* Salvador-BA: Fundação Lar Harmonia, 2004

BOZZANO, Ernesto. *A Crise da Morte.* 4ª. Edição, FEB, Rio de Janeiro-RJ. 1962

BOZZANO, Ernesto. *Animismo ou Espiritismo?.* 2ª. Edição. Rio de Janeiro-RJ: Federação Espírita Brasileira, 1951.

CAMARGO, Pedro de. *O Mestre na Educação.* Rio de Janeiro-RJ: Federação Espírita Brasileira, 1991.

CID, Carlos & Riu, Manoel. *Historia de las Religiones.* Barcelona, Spain: Editorial Ramon Sopena S/A, 1965.

DELANNE, Gabriel. *Evolução Anímica.* 16ª edição. Rio de Janeiro-RJ: Federação Espírita Brasileira, 1976

DENIS, Léon. *Après la Mort.* Paris-France: Dervy-Livres, 1977.

DAWKINS, Richard. *O Gene egoísta.* Lisboa-Portugal: Editora Gradiva, 1989.

EHRENWALD, Jan. *Telepatia y Relaciones Interpersonales.* Buenos Aires-Argentina: Editorial Paidós, Buenos Aires, Argentina, 1961.

FREIRE, Antonio J. *Da Alma Humana.* Rio de Janeiro-RJ: Federação Espírita Brasileira, 1956.

GREEN, Brian. 2001, O Universo Elegante, 5ª. edição, Companhia das Letras, São Paulo, Brazil.

HAWKING, Stephen. *O Universo numa Casca de Noz.* 9ª. Edição. São Paulo-SP: Editora ARX, 2006.

JUNG, Carl G. *The Zofingia Lectures.* Princeton-NJ: Universty Press, Princeton, 1983.

JUNG, Carl G. *Sincronicidade.* O. C., vol. 8/3. Petrópolis-RJ: Editora Vozes, 2005.

JUNG, Carl G. *Cartas.* Vol. II. Petrópolis-RJ: Editora Vozes, 2002.

JUNG, Carl G. *A Natureza da Psique.* O. C., vol. 8/2. Petrópolis-RJ: Editora Vozes, 1984.

KAKU, Michi. *Hiperespaço*. Rio de Janeiro-RJ: Editora Rocco, 2000

KARDEC, Allan. *O Livro dos Espíritos*. Salvador-BA: Fundação Lar Harmonia, 2007.

KARDEC, Allan. *O Livro dos Médiuns*. Salvador-BA: Fundação Lar Harmonia, 2012.
KARDEC, Allan. A Gênese. Brasília-DF: Federação Espírita Brasileira, 2013.

KELLER, Werner. *La Parapsychologie Ouvre le Futur*. Paris-France: Ed. Robert Laffont, 1975.

MONOD, Jacques. 1970, O Acaso e a Necessidade, Editora Vozes, 4ª. Edição, Petrópolis, Brazil.

NOVAES, Adenáuer. 2004, Filosofia e Espiritualidade, Salvador-BA: Fundação Lar Harmonia, 2004.

ROUSTAING, J. B. *Os Quatro Evangelho*s. Quatro volumes. Rio de Janeiro, RJ: Federação Espírita Brasileira, 1971.

RUCKER, Rudy. *A Quarta Dimensão*. Lisboa- Portugal: Gradiva,1991.

SANTOS, Jorge Andréa. *Enfoques Científicos na Doutrina Espírita*. Rio de Janeiro-RJ: Federação Espírita Brasileira, 1987

SEGRÈ, Emilio. *Dos Raios X aos Quarks*. Brasília-DF: Editora Universidade de Brasília, 1987.

SMITH, E. Lester. *Intelligence Came First*. Wheaton – USA: The Theosofical Publishing House, 1975.

UBALDI, Pietro. *A Grande Síntese.* Traduzida por Guillon Ribeiro. Rio de Janeiro-RJ: Livraria da Federação Espírita Brazileira, 1939.

UBALDI, Pietro. *Deus e Universo.* 2 ª edição, Campos-RJ: FUNDAPU, 1984.

WENDT, Herbertd. *A Procura de Adão.* São Paulo-SP: Edições Melhoramentos, 1956.

XAVIER, Francisco Cândido. *Nosso Lar*. 35ª. Edição. Rio de Janeiro-RJ: Federação Espírita Brasileira, 1988

XAVIER, Francisco Cândido. *Os Mensageiros*. Rio de Janeiro-RJ: Federação Espírita Brasileira, 1987.

XAVIER, Francisco Cândido. *Missionários da Luz*. 15ª. edição, Rio de Janeiro-RJ: Federação Espírita Brasileira, 1982.

XAVIER, Francisco Cândido. Libertação, Rio de Janeiro-RJ: Federação Espírita Brasileira,1985.

XAVIER, Francisco Cândido. *Nos domínios da Mediunidade*. 6ª. Edição, Rio de Janeiro-RJ: Federação Espírita Brasileira, 1970.

XAVIER, Francisco Cândido. *Evolução em Dois Mundos*. 8ª. Edição, Rio de Janeiro-RJ: Federação Espírita Brasileira, 1985.

XAVIER, Francisco Cândido. *Mecanismos da Mediunidade*, Rio de Janeiro-RJ: Federação Espírita Brasileira, 1987.

XAVIER, Francisco Cândido .2003, Emmanuel, 22ª. Edição, Rio de Janeiro-RJ: Federação Espírita Brasileira, 2003

ZÖLLNER. Friedrich. 1980, Provas Científicas da Sobrevivência, 4ª. Edição, Edicel, São Paulo, Brazil.